META-ANALYTIC PROCEDURES FOR SOCIAL RESEARCH

Applied Social Research Methods Series
Volume 6

Applied Social Research Methods Series

Series Editor:
LEONARD BICKMAN, Peabody College, Vanderbilt University

Series Associate Editor:
DEBRA ROG, Joint Legislative Audit and
Review Commission, Commonwealth of Virginia

This series is designed to provide students and practicing professionals in the social sciences with relatively inexpensive softcover textbooks describing the major methods used in applied social research. Each text introduces the reader to the state of the art of that particular method and follows step-by-step procedures in its explanation. Each author describes the theory underlying the method to help the student understand the reasons for undertaking certain tasks. Current research is used to support the author's approach. Examples of utilization in a variety of applied fields, as well as sample exercises, are included in the books to aid in classroom use.

Volumes in this series:

1. **SURVEY RESEARCH METHODS,** Floyd J. Fowler, Jr.
2. **THE INTEGRATIVE RESEARCH REVIEW: A Systematic Approach,** Harris M. Cooper
3. **METHODS FOR POLICY RESEARCH,** Ann Majchrzak
4. **SECONDARY RESEARCH: Information Sources and Methods,** David W. Stewart
5. **CASE STUDY RESEARCH: Design and Methods,** Robert K. Yin
6. **META-ANALYTIC PROCEDURES FOR SOCIAL RESEARCH,** Robert Rosenthal

Additional volumes currently in development

META-ANALYTIC PROCEDURES FOR SOCIAL RESEARCH

Robert Rosenthal

Applied Social Research Methods Series
Volume 6

 SAGE PUBLICATIONS Beverly Hills London New Delhi

To MaryLu, Roberta, David, and Virginia
for their combined level of significance

For information address:

SAGE Publications, Inc.
275 South Beverly Drive
Beverly Hills, California 90212

SAGE Publications India Pvt. Ltd.
C-236 Defence Colony
New Delhi 110 024, India

SAGE Publications Ltd
28 Banner Street
London EC1Y 8QE, England

Printed in the United States of America

Library of Congress Cataloging in Publication Data

Rosenthal, Robert, 1933-
    Meta-analytic procedures for social research.

    (Applied social science research methods series ; v. 6)
    Bibliography: p.
    Includes index.
    1. Social sciences—Research. I. Title. II. Series.
H62.R6565   1984   300'.72   84-9821
ISBN 0-8039-2033-4
ISBN 0-8039-2034-2 (pbk.)

FIRST PRINTING

CONTENTS

PREFACE

My interest in meta-analysis grew out of a research result I couldn't quite believe. For reasons chronicled elsewhere (Rosenthal, in press b), I conducted some studies to investigate the effect of psychological experimenters' expectations on the responses obtained from their research subjects. These studies suggested that experimenters' expectations might indeed affect the results of their research. In the late 1950s that result was not very plausible — not to me and not to my colleagues.

A long series of replications followed which eventually persuaded me that there must be something to the phenomenon of interpersonal expectations. Since the early 1960s I have been combining and comparing the results of series of research studies dealing with experimenters' and others' expectations (Rosenthal, 1961, 1963). The basic quantitative procedures for combining and comparing research results were available even then (Mosteller & Bush, 1954; Snedecor, 1956).

In the mid-1960s I began teaching a variety of meta-analytic procedures in courses on research methods though they were not then called meta-analytic. Neither this teaching nor my writing employing meta-analytic procedures seemed to have much effect on the probability of others' employing these procedures. What *did* have an effect on others' employing meta-analytic procedures was an absolutely brilliant paper by Gene V Glass (1976a, 1976b). In this paper, Glass named the summarizing enterprise as "meta-analysis" and gave an elegant example of a way of doing a meta-analysis. In the process, he persuaded me, a former psychotherapist, that I probably *had* helped those patients I'd thought I'd helped.

Since this early work by Glass, and the subsequent work with his colleagues frequently cited in this book, there has been an extraordinary rate of production of meta-analytic research. Since the late 1970s, there have been hundreds of published and unpublished meta-analyses.

The table of contents and the introductory chapter tell in detail what is in this book. Its purpose, very briefly, is to describe meta-analytic procedures in sufficient detail so that they can be carried out by readers of this book and so that they can be wisely evaluated when they have been carried out by others.

The book was designed to be used by advanced undergraduate students, graduate students, and researchers in the social and behavioral sciences. The level of mathematical sophistication required is high school algebra. The level of statistical sophistication required is about half-way through a second course in data analysis (e.g., Rosenthal and Rosnow, 1984a).

I am doubly grateful to the National Science Foundation: first, for having supported, since 1961, the substantive research on interpersonal expectations—the research that gave me something to meta-analyze; and second, for having supported in part the development of some of the methodological procedures to be described in this book.

Let me also thank especially these people: Frederick Mosteller for having markedly enlarged my horizons about meta-analytic procedures some 20 years ago; Jacob Cohen, a fine colleague I have never met, but whose writings about power and effect size estimation have influenced me profoundly; and Donald B. Rubin, a frequent collaborator and my long standing tutor on matters meta-analytic and otherwise quantitative. I have described our collaboration to students as follows: "I ask him questions and he answers them." Clearly, the ideal collaboration!

The manuscript was improved greatly by the suggestions of Len Bickman, Debra Rog, Harris Cooper, and an anonymous reviewer, and it was superbly typed by Blair Boudreau whose legendary accuracy ruins one's skill at, and motivation for, proofreading.

Finally, I thank MaryLu Rosenthal for what she taught me about bibliographic retrieval in the social sciences (M. Rosenthal, 1984) and for the countless ways in which she improved the book and its author.

1

Introduction

Two sources of pessimism in the social sciences are discussed. Early examples of meta-analytic procedures are given that illustrate (1) summarizing relationships, (2) determining moderator variables, and (3) establishing relationships by aggregate analysis. The current status of meta-analytic procedures is described and an empirical evaluation of the employment of meta-analytic procedures is provided.

There is a chronic pessimistic feeling in the social and behavioral sciences that, when compared to the natural sciences, our progress has been exceedingly slow, if indeed there has been any progress at all. From time to time this chronic state erupts into an acute condition, or crisis, precipitated in part by "local" (i.e., disciplinary) developments. For example, in the discipline of social psychology, the precipitating factors leading to prolonged crisis have been brilliantly analyzed by Ralph Rosnow (1981) in his recent book, *Paradigms in Transition*. It seems a good bet, however, that had we been doing better as a science on a chronic basis, our acute crisis would have been less severe. Two *general* purposes of this book are to describe quantitative procedures that will show (1) how we can "do better" than we have been doing, and (2) how we have, in fact, been "doing better" than we think we have been doing.

I. TWO SOURCES OF PESSIMISM IN THE SOCIAL SCIENCES[1]

I.A. Poor Cumulation

One of the two sources of pessimism in the social sciences, the one which is the focus of this book, is the problem of poor cumulation. This problem refers to the observation that the social sciences do not show the orderly progress and development shown by such older sciences as physics and chemistry. The newer work of the physical sciences builds directly upon the older work of those sciences. The social sciences, on the other hand, seem almost to be starting anew with each succeeding volume of our scientific journals.

Poor cumulation does not seem to be due primarily to lack of replication or failure to recognize the need for replication. Indeed, the calls for further research with which we so frequently end our articles are carried wherever our scholarly journals are read. It seems rather that we have been better at issuing such calls than at knowing what to do with the answers. There are many areas of the social sciences for which we do have the results of many studies all addressing essentially the same question. Our summaries of the results of these sets of studies, however, have not been nearly as informative as they might have been, either with respect to summarized significance levels or with respect to summarized effect sizes. Even the best reviews of research by the most sophisticated workers have rarely told us more about each study in a set of studies than the direction of the relationship between the variables investigated and whether or not a given p level was attained. This state of affairs is beginning to change. More and more reviews of the literature are moving from the traditional literary format to the quantitative format (for overviews see Cooper, 1984; Glass, McGaw, & Smith, 1981; Hunter, Schmidt, & Jackson, 1982; Rosenthal, 1980).

Three more *specific* purposes of this book relevant to the problem of poor cumulation include the following:

(1) Defining the concept of a study's "results" more clearly than is our custom in the social sciences.
(2) Providing a general framework for conceptualizing meta-analysis, i.e., the quantitative summary of research domains.
(3) Illustrating the quantitative procedures within this framework so they can be applied by the reader and/or understood more clearly when applied by others.

I.B. Small Effects

The second source of pessimism in the social sciences on which we focus in this book is the problem of *small effects*. Even when we do seem to come up with a possibly replicable result, the practical magnitude of the effect is almost always small, i.e., accounts for only a trivial proportion of the variance. Thus, the complaint goes, even if some social action program works, or if some new teaching method works, or if psychotherapy works, the size of the effect is likely to be so small that it is of no practical consequence whatever.

One specific purpose of this book is to describe a procedure for helping us to evaluate the social importance of the effects of any independent variable. This is done in detail in the final chapter.

II. EARLY EXAMPLES OF
META-ANALYTIC PROCEDURES

Early applications of meta-analytic procedures were of three types. The first type was that in which the goal was to summarize for a set of studies what the overall relationship was between two variables that had been investigated in each study. Often this goal was approached by trying to estimate the average relationship between two variables found in a set of studies. Often this goal was approached by significance testing, i.e., by trying to determine the probability that the relationship obtained could have been obtained if, in the population from which the studies had been sampled, the true relationship were zero.

The second type of early application of meta-analytic procedures was not so much concerned with summarizing the relationship between two variables, but with determining the factors that were associated with *variations* in the magnitude of relationships between the two variables (i.e., the factors that served as moderator variables).

The third type of early application did not examine any relationship within each study. Instead, each study provided only aggregated data for each variable, for instance, the average attitude held by the participants in a study or their average level of cognitive performance. These aggregated or averaged data were then correlated with each other or with other characteristics of the study to test hypotheses or to suggest hypotheses to be tested in subsequent specifically designed studies.

To summarize the differences among these three types of early application of meta-analytic procedures we can say that: (1) the first type generally resulted in an estimate of the average correlation (or the combined p level associated with that correlation) found in all the studies summarized; (2) the second generally resulted in a correlation between some characteristic of the studies and the correlation (or other index of the size of the effect) found in the studies; and (3) the third simply correlated mean data obtained from each study with other mean data or with other characteristics obtained from each study. We turn now to some examples of these three types of early application.

II.A. Summarizing Relationships

One of our early examples is drawn not from social but from agricultural science. Jay Lush (1931) investigated the relationship between the initial weight of steers and their subsequent gain in weight. Lush had six samples of steers available and he was interested in computing the average of the six correlations he had available (median r = .39).

What made these six samples of steers famous was not Lush's averaging of correlations, but George Snedecor's (1946) putting the six correlations into his classic textbook of statistics as an example of how to combine correlation coefficients. Subsequent editions have retained that famous example (e.g., Snedecor & Cochran, 1980). Snedecor's long-time coauthor William G. Cochran had himself been a pioneer in the field of meta-analysis. Early on he had addressed himself to the statistical issues involved in comparing and combining the results of series of studies (Cochran, 1937, 1943).

In his textbook example, Snedecor (1946) did much more than show how to combine estimates of magnitudes of relationships (r's). He also showed how to assess the heterogeneity of a set of correlation coefficients. That is, he showed how a χ^2 test could be employed to help us judge whether, overall, the correlations differed significantly from each other.

Moving from an agricultural to a social science example, my own early meta-analytic research was also concerned with estimating average correlations. In one summary of what was then known about the effects of experimenters' expectancies on the results of their research, the average correlations (based on a number of studies each based on a number of experimenters) were reported between experimenters' expectancies for their subjects performance and how their subjects subsequently did perform (Rosenthal, 1961, 1963). These average correlations were computed separately for experimenters who were explicitly encouraged to bias their results (median r = $-.21$) and those who were not (median r = .43). A test (contrast) was then performed to help judge whether these average correlations differed significantly from each other. They did differ, suggesting that, while under ordinary circumstances experimenters tended to get the results they expected to get, they tended to get significantly opposite results when they felt unduly influenced (or even bribed) to bias the results of their research (Rosenthal, 1961, 1963). Analogous analyses were performed on a series of studies investigating the relationship between experimenters' personality and the extent to which they obtained data affected by their expectancy (Rosenthal, 1961, 1963, 1964).

Snedecor's textbook example of testing for the heterogeneity of a set of correlation coefficients was also applied to the study of experimenter effects. In one such analysis, eight studies could be found in which experimenters had served as subjects in the same task they were now administering to others in their role of experimenter. The correlations could therefore be obtained between the performance of experimenters at a given task and the average performance of those experimenters' subjects on the same task. The application of Snedecor's test showed the eight correlation coefficients to be significantly heterogenous (Rosenthal, 1961, 1963).

Snedecor's textbook example illustrated both the computation of average r's and a test for heterogeneity of r's. What his example did not illustrate was an overall test of significance to help us judge the probability that the particular set of r's with their associated tests of significance could have been obtained if the true value of r in the appropriate population were zero. Had Snedecor wanted he could readily have illustrated the process of combining probability levels. At least two major figures in the history of mathematical statistics, Ronald Fisher (e.g., 1932, 1938) and Karl Pearson (1933a, 1933b) had already described procedures for combining probabilities. Even earlier, Tippett (1931) had described a related procedure that did not exactly combine probabilities but "protected" the smallest obtained p by multiplying it by the number of tests of significance examined.

Mosteller and Bush (1954) broadened the Fisher and Pearson perspectives and made several methods of combining independent probabilities available to social scientists in general and to social psychologists in particular. An early and ingenious application of a method of combining probabilities was described by Stouffer and his colleagues (1949). For three samples of male soldiers, data were available on the favorability of their view of women soldiers as a function of the presence of women soldiers at their own camp. Male soldiers tended to be more unfavorable to women soldiers (as defined by not wanting their sisters to join the Army) when women soldiers were at their camp.

Returning to our examples of studies of experimenter expectancy effects we find illustrations of the application of the Stouffer method of combining probabilities. After the first three experiments showed the effects of experimentally-created expectations on the results of their research, the three probability levels obtained were combined to give an overall test of significance for the set of three studies (Rosenthal, 1966).

II.B. Determining Moderator Variables

In this section we describe an early application of meta-analytic procedures in which the goal was not to establish an overall relationship between two variables, but to determine the factors that were associated with variations in the magnitudes of the relationships between two variables. Such factors are known as moderator variables because they moderate or alter the magnitude of a relationship.

An early application was by Thorndike (1933). He obtained the results of 36 independent studies of the retest reliability of the Binet test of intelligence. Thorndike was not interested in an overall estimate of the retest reliability per se, but in how the magnitude of the retest reliability correlation varied as a function of the time interval between the first and second testing. As might be expected, the greater the interval, the lower the retest reliability. These intervals ranged from less than one month to 60 months with a median interval of about two years.

Thorndike did not report an overall estimate of the retest reliability (r = .84) or the correlation between the magnitude of the retest reliability and the retest time interval ($r(34) = -.39$). He did report the estimated reliabilities separately for various retest intervals; e.g., less than one month ($r = .95$) to nearly five years ($r = .81$). (The average reliabilities reported here are not those reported by Thorndike but are corrected estimates.)

A somewhat later example of the use of moderator variables is drawn from the research program on experimenter effects mentioned earlier. Eight studies had been summarized in each of which the performance of experimenters at a given task could be correlated with the average performance of those experimenters' subjects on the same task. Rosenthal (1963, 1964) was interested in learning the degree to which these correlations changed from the earlier to the later studies. He found a significant and substantial ($r = .81$) effect of *when* the study was done; studies conducted earlier obtained significantly more positive correlations (relative to later-conducted studies) while later-conducted studies obtained more negative correlations (relative to earlier-conducted studies).

II.C. Establishing Relationships by Aggregate Analysis

In this section we describe an early application of the meta-analytic procedure wherein each study provides only aggregated (average) data for each variable.

Underwood (1957) was interested in the relationship between the degree of retention of various kinds of learned materials (e.g., geometric forms, nonsense syllables, nouns) and the number of previous lists of materials that had been learned. He hypothesized that the more lists that had been learned before the recall tests, the greater would be the forgetting. Underwood found 14 studies that each yielded both required facts: percentage recalled after 24 hours and the average number of previoiusly learned lists. His hypothesis was strongly supported by the data. The correlation between these two variables (r based on ranks) was dramatically large: $r(12) = -.91$! (We would not expect fo find correlations that large within the individual studies contributing to the aggregate analysis, however, since it is characteristic of aggregate analyses to yield larger correlations.)

II.D. Summarizing, Moderating, and Establishing Relationships Meta-Analytically

As a review of the differences among the early meta-analytic procedures designed for the three different purposes we have illustrated so far, Table 1.1 has been prepared, a hypothetical example illustrating differences in summarizing relationships, determining moderator variables, and establishing relationships. Column A shows the results of six studies of teacher expectancy effects expressed for each study as the correlation between teacher expectations and pupil performance. Column B shows the mean rating of the

TABLE 1.1
Illustration of Differences in Summarizing Relationships, Determining Moderator Variables, and Establishing Relationships

Study	A Correlations Between Teacher Expectations and Pupil Performance (r)	B Mean Ratings of Teacher Excellence	C Mean Level of Pupil Performance
1	.25	8	115
2	.20	9	110
3	.30	9	105
4	.35	7	105
5	.15	6	100
6	.10	5	95
Mean	.22	7.3	105.0

NOTES: The mean of column A illustrates the summarizing function; the correlation between columns A and B (r = .59) (and A and C; r = .53) illustrates the examination of moderator variables; and the correlation between columns B and C illustrates the attempt to establish a relationship (r = .78). This table represents only a hypothetical example.

excellence of the teachers employed in each of the six studies. Column C shows the mean level of pupil performance found for all the children of each of the six studies.

The summarizing function of meta-analysis is illustrated by the mean of Column A, i.e., the mean magnitude of the relationship between teacher expectations and pupil performance.

The determination of moderator variables is illustrated by the correlation of the data in Column A and the data in Column B. That correlation (r = .59) shows that larger effects of teacher expectations are associated with teachers who have on the average been judged to be more excellent. Another illustration of moderating effects is found in the correlation between Column A and Column C. That correlation (r = .53) shows that larger effects of teacher expectations are associated with pupils who have on the average shown higher levels of performance.

The attempt to establish a relation by aggregate analysis is illustrated by the correlation of Columns B and C. That correlation (r = .78) shows that higher levels of mean pupil performance are associated with higher levels of rated teacher excellence. It might be tempting to interpret this correlation to mean that better teachers produce higher levels of pupil performance but that cannot properly be inferred from the correlation obtained. It would take a freshly designed study to establish properly the causal factors, if any, contributing to the obtained correlation. Similarly, the correlations describing the operation of moderator variables cannot be interpreted causally in most cases since we did not randomly assign studies to the various levels of the moderator variables. Cooper (1984) has made this point clearly and forcefully in his new book in this series. Causal inferences, however, can be made about the results of the studies being summarized if these results are based on experiments involving random assignment of subjects to treatment conditions.

III. THE CURRENT STATUS OF
META-ANALYTIC PROCEDURES

We have now examined several early examples of meta-analytic procedures, some going back over half a century. Although several of the procedures have been available for many years (the present writer has been employing some for over 20 years), there has been no revolution in how we conduct reviews of the literature or summarize domains of research. That is, most reviews of the literature still follow a more traditional narrative style. However, there may be a revolution in the making. As evidence, consider that in their analysis of the number of publications on meta-analysis from the years 1976 to 1982, Lamb and Whitla (1983) found a strong linear increase ($r = .85$) from the 6 papers of 1976 to the 120 papers of 1982.

The work that probably did the most to capture the imagination of the social sciences as to the value of meta-analytic procedures was the brilliant meta-analytic work of Gene Glass and his collaborators. Specifically, Glass and his colleagues, employing meta-analytic procedures very similar to those of the present writer (Rosenthal, 1961, 1963, 1969, 1976; Rosenthal & Rosnow, 1975) but developed independently, were able to demonstrate dramatically the effectiveness of psychotherapy (Glass, 1976a, 1976b, 1977; Smith & Glass, 1977; Smith, Glass, & Miller, 1980). Partly because of the work of Glass and his group, the last few years have shown a rapidly growing number of investigators who have been discussing, employing, and developing a variety of meta-analytic procedures. These investigators include Bloom, 1964; Cook & Leviton, 1980; Cooper, 1979, 1982, 1984; Cooper & Rosenthal, 1980; DePaulo, Zuckerman, & Rosenthal, 1980; Dusek & Joseph, 1983; Eagly & Carli, 1981; Feldman, 1971; Fiske, 1983; Glass, 1976, 1980; Glass & Kliegl, 1983; Glass et al., 1981; Green & Hall, in press; Hall, 1980; Hedges, 1981, 1982a, 1982b, 1982c, 1983a, 1983b; Hedges & Olkin, 1980, 1982, 1983a, 1983b; Hunter et al., 1982; Kulik, Kulik, & Cohen, 1979; Light, 1979; Light & Pillemer, 1982; Light & Smith, 1971; Mintz, 1983; Mullen & Rosenthal, 1983; Pillemer & Light, 1980a, 1980b; Rosenthal, 1963, 1964, 1968, 1969, 1976, 1978, 1979, 1980, 1982, 1983a, 1983b, 1983c, in press-a, in press-b; Rosenthal & DePaulo, 1979; Rosenthal & Rosnow, 1975; Rosenthal & Rubin, 1978, 1979a, 1980, 1982b, 1982c, 1983, in press; Shapiro & Shapiro, 1983; Smith, 1980; Smith & Glass, 1977; Smith et al., 1980; Strube & Hartman, 1983; Sudman & Bradburn, 1974; Taveggia, 1974; Viana, 1980; Walberg & Haertel, 1980; Wilson

Quite Mrs Fields

(Anne)

& Rachman, 1983; Zuckerman, DePaulo, & Rosenthal, 1981 and the many others cited in the references of these workers.

In the pages that lie ahead we consider in detail how to employ a variety of meta-analytic procedures. Our procedures are not perfect, we can use them inappropriately, and we will make mistakes. Nevertheless, the alternative to the systematic, explicit, quantitative procedures to be described is even less perfect, even more likely to be applied inappropriately, and even more likely to lead us to error. There is nothing in the set of meta-analytic procedures that makes us less able to engage in creative thought. All the thoughtful and intuitive procedures of the traditional review of the literature can also be employed in a meta-analytic review. However, meta-analytic reviews go beyond the traditional reviews in the degree to which they are more systematic, more explicit, more exhaustive, and more quantitative. Because of these features, meta-analytic reviews are more likely to lead to summary statements of greater thoroughness, greater precision, and greater intersubjectivity or objectivity (Kaplan, 1964). In the final chapter of this book we consider systematically the several criticisms that have been made of meta-analytic procedures and products.

IV. AN EMPIRICAL EVALUATION
OF META-ANALYTIC PROCEDURES

Harris Cooper and I were interested in assessing empirically the effects of employing meta-analytic procedures on the conclusions drawn by investigators in training (i.e., graduate students) and experienced investigators (i.e., faculty members) (Cooper & Rosenthal, 1980). The basic idea was to ask the participants to conduct a review of the literature to address the question of sex differences in task persistence. Some of the participants were randomly assigned to the meta-analytic procedure condition, and some were randomly assigned to the traditional procedure condition. All of the participants were given the same seven studies that we knew beforehand significantly supported overall the hypothesis that females showed greater task persistence.

There was a total of 41 participants initially blocked on sex and faculty (versus graduate student) status. However, since neither of these variables affected the results of the experiment, results were reported for all 41 participants combined. Participants assigned to the meta-analytic procedure condition were asked to record the significance level of each study and were given detailed instructions on how to combine these significance levels to obtain an overall test of significance for the entire set of seven studies. Participants assigned to the traditional procedure condition were asked to employ whatever procedures they would normally employ to conduct a review of the literature.

After participants completed their reviews, they were asked whether the evidence supported the conclusion that females were more task persistent than males. They could respond: definitely yes, probably yes, can't tell, probably no, or definitely no. Participants were also asked to estimate the magnitude of the relationship between gender and persistence. To this question they could respond: none at all, very small, small, moderate, large, and very large.

Despite the fact that the set of seven studies reviewed showed a clearly significant relationship between sex and task persistence, 73% of the traditional reviewers found probably or definitely no support for the hypothesis compared to only 32% of the meta-analytic reviewers. That difference (significant at $p < .005$), suggests that traditional methods of reviewing may suffer a very considerable loss of power relative to meta-analytic methods. Put another way, the incidence of type II errors (failing to reject null hypotheses that are false) may be far greater for the traditional than for the meta-analytic procedures of summarizing research domains.

NOTE

1. Throughout this book reference to the social sciences or to the behavioral sciences will refer to both the social and behavioral sciences.

2

Defining Research Results

The concept of "research results" is clarified and the relationship between tests of significance and estimates of effect sizes is emphasized. Various types of effect size estimates and adjustments of these estimates are described. Finally, five methods of dealing with the problem of multiple correlated results are outlined.

Much of the rest of this book will deal with quantitative procedures for comparing and combining the results of a series of studies. Before these procedures can be discussed meaningfully, however, we must become explicit about what we mean when we refer to the results of an individual study.

We begin by stating what we do *not* mean when we refer to the results of a study: We do not mean the conclusion drawn by the investigator, since that is often only vaguely related to the actual results. The metamorphosis that sometimes occurs between the results section and the discussion section is itself a topic worthy of detailed consideration. For now it is enough to note that a fairly ambiguous result often becomes quite smooth and rounded in the discussion section, so that reviewers who dwell too much on the discussion and too little on the results can be quite misled as to what actually was found.

We also do not mean the result of an omnibus F test with df > 1 in the numerator or an omnibus χ^2 test with df > 1. In both cases we are getting quantitative answers to questions that are often—perhaps usually—hopelessly imprecise. Only rarely is one interested in knowing for any fixed-factor analysis of variance or covariance that somewhere in the thicket of df there lurk one or more meaningful answers to meaningful questions that we had not the foresight to ask of our data. Similarly, there are few occasions when what we really want to know is that somewhere in a contingency table there is an obtained frequency or two that has strayed too far from the frequency expected for that cell under the null hypothesis.

What we shall mean by the results is the answer to this question: What is the relationship between any variable X and any variable Y? The variables X and Y are chosen with only the constraint that their relationship be of interest to us. The answer to this question must come in two parts: (1) the estimate of the magnitude of the relationship (the effect size) and (2) an indication of the accuracy or reliability of the estimated effect size (as in a confidence interval placed around the estimate). An alternative to the second part of the answer is one not intrinsically more useful but one more consistent with the existing practices of social researchers, that is, the test of significance of the difference between the obtained effect size and the effect size expected under the null hypothesis of no relationship between variables X and Y.

I. EFFECT SIZE AND STATISTICAL SIGNIFICANCE

Since the argument has been made that the results of a study with respect to any given relationship can be expressed an an estimate of an effect size plus a test of significance, we should make explicit the relationship between these two quantitities. The general relationship is shown below:

Test of Significance	=	Size of Effect	×	Size of Study

Tables 2.1 and 2.2 give useful specific examples of this general equation. Equation 2.1 shows that χ^2 on df $= 1$ is the product of the size of the effect expressed by ϕ^2 (the squared product moment correlation) multiplied by N (the number of subjects or other sampling units). It should be noted that ϕ is merely Pearson's r applied to dichotomous data, i.e., data coded as taking on only two values such as 0 and 1, 1 and 2, or $+1$ and -1.

Equation 2.2 is simply the square root of equation 2.1. It shows that the standard normal deviate Z (i.e., the square root of χ^2 on 1 df) is the product of ϕ (the product moment correlation) and $\sqrt{N}$. Equation 2.3 shows that t is the product of the effect size $r/\sqrt{1-r^2}$ and $\sqrt{df}$, an index of the size of the study. The denominator of this effect size ($\sqrt{1-r^2}$) is also known as the coefficient of alienation or k, an index of the degree of noncorrelation (Guilford & Fruchter, 1978). This effect size, therefore, can be rewritten as r/k, the ratio of correlation to noncorrelation. Equations 2.4 and 2.5 share the same effect size, the difference between the means of the two compared groups divided by, or standardized by, the unbiased estimate of the population standard deviation.

TABLE 2.1
Examples of the Relationship Between Tests of Significance and Effect Size: $\chi^2(1)$, Z, and t

Equation	Test of Significance	=	Size of Effect	×	Size of Study
2.1	$\chi^2(1)$	=	Φ^2	×	N
2.2	Z	=	Φ	×	$\sqrt{N}$
2.3	t	=	$\dfrac{r}{\sqrt{1-r^2}}$	×	$\sqrt{df}$
2.4	t	=	$\left(\dfrac{M_1-M_2}{S}\right)^a$	×	$\dfrac{1}{\sqrt{\dfrac{1}{n_1}+\dfrac{1}{n_2}}}$
2.5	t	=	$\left(\dfrac{M_1-M_2}{S}\right)^a$	×	$\sqrt{\dfrac{n_1 n_2}{n_1 + n_2}}$
2.6	t	=	$\left(\dfrac{M_1-M_2}{\sigma}\right)^b$	×	$\left[\dfrac{\sqrt{n_1 n_2}}{(n_1 + n_2)} \times \sqrt{df}\right]$
2.7	t	=	d	×	$\dfrac{\sqrt{df}}{2}$

a. Also called g (Hedges, 1981, 1982a).
b. Also called d (Cohen, 1969, 1977).

TABLE 2.2
Examples of the Relationship Between Tests of Significance and Effect Size: F and t for Correlated Observations

Equation	Test of Significance	=	Size of Effect	×	Size of Study
2.8	F[a]	=	$\dfrac{r^2}{1-r^2}$	×	df error
2.9	F[b]	=	$\dfrac{eta^2}{1 - eta^2}$	×	$\dfrac{df\ error}{df\ means}$
2.10	F[b]	=	$\dfrac{S^2\ means}{S^2}$	×	n
2.11	t[c]	=	$\dfrac{r}{\sqrt{1 - r^2}}$	×	$\sqrt{df}$
2.12	t[c]	=	$\dfrac{\bar{D}}{S_D}$	×	$\sqrt{n}$
2.13	t[c]	=	d	×	$\sqrt{df}$

a. Numerator df = 1.
b. numerator df may take on any value.
c. Correlated observations.

This latter effect size $(M_1 - M_2)/S$ is the one typically employed by Glass and his colleagues (1981) with the S computed as $[\Sigma (X - \bar{X})^2/(n_c - 1)]^{1/2}$ employing only the subjects or other sampling units from the *control group*. The pooled S—that is, the one computed from both groups—tends to provide a better estimate in the long run of the population standard deviation. However, when the S's based on the two different conditions differ greatly from each other, choosing the control group S as the standardizing quantity is a very reasonable alternative. That is because it is always possible that the experimental treatment itself has made the S of the experimental group too large or too small relative to the S of the control group.

Another alternative when the S's of the two groups differ greatly is to transform the data to make the S's more similar. Such transformations (e.g., logs, square roots, etc.) of course require our having access to the original data, but that is also often required to compute S separately for the control group. When only a mean square error from an analysis of variance is available we must be content to use its square root (S) as our standardizing denominator in any case. Or if only the results of a t test are given, we are similarly forced to compute the effect size using a pooled estimate of S. (We could use equations 2.4 or 2.5 to solve for $(M_1 - M_2)/S$.)

Before leaving the topic of whether to compute S only from the control group or from both groups we should remind ourselves of the following: When S's differ greatly for the two groups so that we are inclined to compute S only from the control group, ordinary t tests may give misleading results. Such problems can be approached by approximate procedures (Snedecor & Cochran, 1980, pp. 96–98) but are perhaps best dealt with by appropriate transformation of the data (Tukey, 1977).

Equation 2.6 shows an effect size only slightly different from that of equations 2.4 and 2.5. The only difference is that the standardizing quantity for the difference between the means is s (pooled sums of squares divided by N) rather than S (pooled sums of squares divided by N − k for k groups). This is one of the effect sizes employed by Cohen (1969, 1977) and by Friedman (1968). Basically this index, Cohen's d, is the difference between the means of the groups being compared given in standard score units or z-scores. Equation 2.7 shows $(M_1 - M_2)/\sigma$ expressed as d and the size of study term simplified considerably for those situations in which it is known or in which it can be reasonably assumed that the sample sizes (n_1 and n_2) are equal.

Equation 2.8 of Table 2.2 shows that F with one df in the numerator is the product of the squared ingredients of the right hand side of equation 2.3 of Table 2.1. That is just as it should be, of course, given that $t^2 = F$ when df = 1 in the numerator of F.

Equation 2.9 is the generalization of equation 2.8 to the situation of df > 1 in the numerator. Thus eta^2 refers to the proportion of variance accounted for just as r^2 does, but eta^2 carries no implication that the relationship between the two variables in question is linear. Equation 2.10 shows the effect size for F as the ratio of the variance of the condition means to the pooled within group variance, while the size of the study is indexed by n, the number of observations in each of the groups. Because we rarely employ fixed effect F tests with df > 1 in the numerator in meta-analytic work, equations 2.9 and 2.10 are used infrequently in summarizing domains of research.

I.A. Comparing r to d

Equation 2.11 has for its test of significance a t for correlated observations or repeated measures. It is important to note that this equation for the correlated t is identical to equation 2.3 (Table 2.1) for the independent samples t. Thus when we employ r as our effect size estimate, we need not make any special adjustment in moving from t tests for independent to those for correlated observations. That is not the situation for equations 2.12 and 2.13, however. When the effect size estimates are the mean differences divided either by S or by σ, the definition of the size of the study changes by a factor of 2 in going from t for independent observations to t for correlated observations. This inconsistency in definitions of size of study is one of the reasons I have recently grown to prefer r as an effect size estimate rather than d, after many years of using both r and d.

Another reason for preferring r over d as an effect size estimate is that we are often unable to compute d accurately from the information provided by the author of the original article. Investigators sometimes report only their t's and df's but not their sample sizes. Therefore, we cannot use equations 2.4, 2.5, or 2.6 to compute the effect sizes. We could do so only if we assumed $n_1 = n_2$. If we did so, for example, from rearranging equation 2.7, we could get d as follows:

$$d = \frac{2t}{\sqrt{df}} \qquad [2.14]$$

If the investigator's sample sizes were equal, d would be accurate, but as n_1 and n_2 become more and more unequal, d will be more and more underestimated. Table 2.3 shows for eight studies, all with t = 3.00 and df = $n_1 + n_2 - 2 = 98$, the increasing underestimation of d when we assume equal n's and employ equation 2.14. It should be noted, however, that when the split is no more extreme than 70:30 the underestimation is less than 8%.

A third reason for preferring r to d as an effect size estimate has to do with simplicity of interpretation in practical terms. In the final chapter of this book we describe the BESD (binomial effect size display), a method for displaying the practical importance of the size of an obtained effect. Using this method we can immediately convert r to an improvement in success rate

TABLE 2.3
Underestimation of d by "Equal n" Formula

Study	n_1	n_2	Accurate d^a	Estimated d^b	Raw Difference	Underestimated (in percentages)
1	50	50	.61	.61	.00	.00
2	60	40	.62	.61	−.01	.02
3	70	30	.66	.61	−.05	.08
4	80	20	.76	.61	−.15	.20
5	90	10	1.01	.61	−.40	.40
6	95	5	1.39	.61	−.78	.56
7	98	2	2.16	.61	−1.55	.72
8	99	1	3.05	.61	−2.44	.80

a. $d = \dfrac{t(n_1 + n_2)}{\sqrt{df}\ \sqrt{n_1 n_2}}$ = General formula from rearranging equation 2.6.

b. $d = \dfrac{2t}{\sqrt{df}}$ = "equal n" formula from rearranging equation 2.7.

associated, for example, with employing a new treatment procedure or a new selection device, or a new predictor variable. Because of the probability of seriously misinterpreting its practical importance (as discussed in Chapter 7), we shall not use r^2 as an effect size estimate (Rosenthal & Rubin, 1982c).

Although I have grown to prefer r over d for the reasons just given, the most important point to be made is that some estimate of the size of the effect should always be given whenever results are reported. Whether we employ r, g, d, Glass's Δ (difference between the means divided by the S computed from the control group only) or any of the other effect size estimates that could be employed (e.g., Cohen, 1977) is less important than that some effect size estimate be employed along with the more traditional test of significance.

I.B. Computing Effect Sizes

The emphasis in this book will be on r as the primary effect size estimate. Since most investigators do not yet routinely provide effect size estimates along with their tests of significance we must usually compute our own from the tests of significance they have provided. The following formulas can be found by rearranging equations 2.1, 2.3, and 2.8 (Cohen, 1965; Friedman, 1968):

$$\phi = \sqrt{\frac{\chi^2(1)}{N}} \qquad [2.15]$$

$$r = \sqrt{\frac{t^2}{t^2 + df}} \qquad [2.16]$$

where $df = n_1 + n_2 - 2$, and

$$r = \sqrt{\frac{F(1,-)}{F(1,-) + df \text{ error}}} \qquad [2.17]$$

where $F(1, -)$ indicates any F with $df = 1$ in the numerator.

In case none of these tests of significance have been employed or reported, we can usefully estimate an effect size r from a p level alone as long as we know the size of the study (N). We convert the obtained p to its standard normal deviate equivalent using a table of Z values. We then find r from:

$$r = \sqrt{\frac{Z^2}{N}} = \frac{Z}{\sqrt{N}} \qquad [2.18]$$

It should be noted that equations 2.15 to 2.18 all yield product moment correlation coefficients. It makes no difference whether the data are in dichotomous or continuous form, or whether they are ranked. Thus correlations known as Pearson's r, Spearman's rho, phi, or point biserial r, are all defined in exactly the same way—though there are computational simplifications available so that some appear to be different from others—and are interpreted in exactly the same way.

If we should want to have r as our effect size estimate when only Cohen's d is available we can readily go to r from d (Cohen, 1977):

$$r = \frac{d}{\sqrt{d^2 + \frac{1}{pq}}} \qquad [2.19]$$

where p is the proportion of the total population that is in the first of the two groups being compared and q is the proportion in the second of the two groups, or $1 - p$. When p and q are equal, or when they can be viewed as equal in principle, equation 2.19 is simplified to equation 2.20.

$$r = \frac{d}{\sqrt{d^2 + 4}} \qquad [2.20]$$

In most experimental applications we use equation 2.20 because we think of equal population sizes in principle. We might prefer equation 2.19 in situations where we have intrinsic inequality of population sizes as when we compare the personal adjustment scores of a random sample of normals and a random sample of hospitalized psychiatric patients.

In those cases where we want to work with Cohen's d but have only r available we can go from r to d:

$$d = \frac{2r}{\sqrt{1 - r^2}}$$

[2.21]

II. INFERENTIAL ERRORS

If the reported results of a study always include both an estimate of effect size and a test of significance (or a related procedure such as a confidence interval) we can better protect ourselves against the inferential invalidity of type I and type II errors. There is little doubt that in the social and behavioral sciences type II errors (concluding that X and Y are unrelated when they really are related) are far more likely than type I errors (Cohen, 1962, 1977). The frequency of type II errors can be reduced drastically by our attention to the magnitude of the estimated effect size. If that estimate is large and we find a nonsignificant result, we would do well to avoid deciding that variables X and Y are not related. Only if the pooled results of a good many replications point to both a very small effect size on the average and to a combined test of significance that does not reach our favorite alpha level are we justified in concluding that no nontrivial relationship exists between X and Y. Table 2.4 summarizes inferential errors and some possible conse-

TABLE 2.4
Population Effect Sizes and Results of Significance Testing
as Determinants of Inferential Errors

Population Effect Size	Results of Significance Testing	
	Not Significant	Significant
Zero	No Error	Type I Error
Small	Type II Error[a]	No Error[b]
Large	Type II Error[c]	No Error

a. Low power may lead to failure to detect the true effect, but if the true effect is quite small the costs of this error may not be too great.
b. Although not an inferential error, if the effect size is *very* small and N is very large we may mistake a result that is merely very significant for one that is of practical importance.
c. Low power may lead to failure to detect the true effect and with a substantial true effect the costs of this error may be very great.

quences as a joint function of the results of significance testing and the population effect size.

III. ADJUSTING EFFECT SIZE ESTIMATES

III.A. The Fisher and the Hedges Adjustments

In this book our primary effect size estimator will be the correlation coefficient r. However, as the population value of r gets further and further from zero the distribution of r's sampled from that population becomes more and more skewed. This fact complicates the comparison and combination of r's, a complication addressed by Fisher (1928). He devised a transformation (z_r) that is distributed nearly normally. In virtually all the meta-analytic procedures we shall be discussing, whenever we are interested in r we shall actually carry out most of our computations not on r but on its transformation z_r. The relationship between r and z_r is given by:

$$z_r = \tfrac{1}{2} \log_e \left[\frac{1 + r}{1 - r} \right] \qquad [2.22]$$

Fisher (1928, p. 172) noted that there was a small and often negligible bias in z_r, each being too large by r-population/$[2(N - 1)]$. Only when N is very small while at the same time the r-population (the actual population value of r) is very substantial is the bias of any consequence. For practical purposes, therefore, it can safely be ignored (Snedecor & Cochran, 1980). Before leaving this introduction to z_r, it should be noted that it would make a very serviceable effect size estimate but one not as easily interpreted as r (see the final chapter).

There are analogous biases in other effect size estimates, such as Glass's Δ, Hedges's g, and Cohen's d; Hedges (1981, 1982a) has provided both exact and approximate correction factors. Hedges's unbiased estimator g^u is given by

$$g^u = c(m)g \qquad [2.23]$$

where g is the effect size estimate computed as $(M_1 - M_2)/S$ (with S computed from both the experimental and the control groups) and c(m) is given approximately by

$$c(m) \approx 1 - \frac{3}{4m - 1} \qquad [2.24]$$

where m is the df computed from both the experimental and control groups or $n_1 + n_2 - 2$.

III.A.1. Illustrating Fisher's and Hedges's adjustments. To illustrate Fisher's and Hedges's methods of adjustment we assume an experiment in which $n_1 = 4$ and $n_2 = 8$ with t (10) = 2.76. To illustrate Fisher's method we need r as our estimate of effect size. Equation 2.3 of Table 2.1 can be used to obtain r by way of equation 2.16. For this example:

$$r = \sqrt{\frac{(2.76)^2}{(2.76)^2 + 10}} = .658; z_r = .789$$

The bias to be corrected in z_r is r-population divided by $2(N - 1)$. Of course, we don't know the r-population, but we can begin by employing the obtained r as a first approximation. We therefore estimate the bias in z_r as

$$\text{estimated bias}_1 = \frac{.658}{2(12 - 1)} = .030$$

This bias is to be removed from the obtained z_r of .789 so our corrected z_r is

$$.789 - .030 = .759$$

which is associated with a corrected r of .640. Since we now have a more accurate estimate of the population value of r (i.e., .640) we could repeat the calculations to obtain a still more accurate correction for bias:

$$\text{estimated bias}_2 = \frac{.640}{2(12 - 1)} = .029$$

This corrected bias differs little from our first approximation and leads to a corrected z_r of

$$.789 - .029 = .760$$

which is associated with a corrected r of .641. Note that the corrected r differs little from the uncorrected r (.658 versus .641) even though N was quite small (12) and r-population was estimated to be quite substantial.

To illustrate Hedges's method of correction for small sample bias we need g as our estimate of effect size. Since g is defined as $(M_1 - M_2)/S$ we can obtain g from equations 2.4 or 2.5 from Table 2.1 as

$$g = t \sqrt{\frac{1}{n_1} + \frac{1}{n_2}} = (2.76) \sqrt{\frac{1}{4} + \frac{1}{8}} = 1.69 \qquad [2.25]$$

or

$$g = \frac{t\sqrt{n_1 + n_2}}{\sqrt{n_1 n_2}} = \frac{(2.76)\sqrt{4+8}}{\sqrt{(4)(8)}} = 1.69 \qquad [2.26]$$

To employ Hedges's approximate correction we obtain g^u as a function of $c(m)$ and g. For this example $m = 4 + 8 - 2 = 10$, so:

$$c(m) \approx 1 - \frac{3}{4(m)-1} = 1 - \frac{3}{39} = .9231$$

and

$$g^u = c(m)g = (.9231)1.69 = 1.56$$

Table 2.5 summarizes Fisher's and Hedges's adjustments for the present example. The reduction in effect size is greater for Hedges's method than for Fisher's method but since the metric r and the metric g are not directly comparable we must first find a common metric before we can interpret the relative magnitude of the corrections made. A suitable common metric is the t distribution on 10 df since both r and g can be expressed in terms of this distribution. The lower half of Table 2.5 shows that, for the present example, Hedges's correction is more extreme than is Fisher's correction, but both corrections are less than 8% in units of the $t(10)$ distribution.

If one should want to convert r to g it can be done as follows:

$$g = \frac{r}{\sqrt{1 - r^2}} \times \sqrt{\frac{df(n_1 + n_2)}{n_1 n_2}} \qquad [2.27]$$

TABLE 2.5
Fisher's and Hedges's Adjustments for Bias

	Effect Sizes	
	r	g
Effect Size		
Original	.658	1.69
Corrected	.641	1.56
Difference	.017	.13
Percentage reduction	2.6	7.7
Location on t(10) Distribution		
Original	2.76	2.76
Corrected	2.64	2.55
Difference	.12	.21
Percentage reduction	4.3	7.6

If one should want to convert g to r it can be done as follows:

$$r = \sqrt{\frac{g^2 n_1 n_2}{g^2 n_1 n_2 + (n_1 + n_2)df}} \qquad [2.28]$$

III.B. The Hunter, Schmidt, and Jackson Adjustments

In addition to the adjustments suggested by Fisher and by Hedges for small sample sizes, Hunter, Schmidt, and Jackson (1982) have suggested that effect sizes be corrected for the unreliability of the two variables being correlated and for the restriction (or enhancement) of the range of the variables involved. These corrections can be useful aids to understanding the results of an analysis, but I recommend that when such corrections are made the uncorrected results should be presented as well. Since correction for attenuation and for range restriction are not routinely employed by social researchers, greater comparability to typical research can be obtained by presenting the uncorrected results.

Adjustments for unreliability and for restriction of range are applied at the level of the individual study. Hunter et al. (1982) also suggest adjustments for sampling error at the level of the meta-analytic set of studies. For example, the effect sizes obtained from each of a set of studies could be correlated with some feature of the study such as the year in which it was conducted, the average age of the subjects involved in each study, and so on. Such correlations can be corrected for sampling error. Which such corrections can be usefully employed, the present writer recommends that the uncorrected correlation always be presented as well.

III.C. The Glass, McGaw, and Smith Adjustments

Studies entering into a meta-analysis differ in the precision of the statistical procedures employed in their analysis. Thus repeated measures designs (of which gain score analyses are a special case), analysis of covariance designs, and designs employing blocking will tend to produce larger effect sizes and more significant test statistics than would the analogous unblocked posttest only designs. Glass, McGaw, and Smith (1981) have shown how we might convert the results of various designs onto a common scale of effect size (e.g., Δ or g) based on the unblocked posttest only. These adjustments cannot always be made for the results of other people's studies, but can often be quite usefully employed. However, when they are employed, I recommend that both the adjusted and unadjusted statistics be reported.

Just as repeated measures, covariance, and blocking designs tend to increase power, the use of nonparametric tests of significance may tend to decrease power, and Glass et al. (1981) provide adjustment procedures. As in the case of adjustments noted earlier, I recommend reporting the unadjusted statistics along with those that have been adjusted. When nonparametric tests have been employed, a useful estimate of effect size (r) can be obtained from looking up the standard normal deviate (Z) associated with the accurately determined p level and finding r from

$$r = \sqrt{\frac{Z^2}{N}} = \frac{Z}{\sqrt{N}} \qquad\qquad [2.18]$$

An alternative procedure that can be used when p is not too low is to find the t(df) that is equivalent to the obtained p and employ

$$r = \sqrt{\frac{t^2}{t^2 + df}} \qquad\qquad [2.16]$$

This equation does not work well when p is very low because most tables of t do not include t's associated with $p < .0001$.

IV. SOME SOLUTIONS TO THE PROBLEM
OF MULTIPLE (CORRELATED) RESULTS

Many of the studies entering into our meta-analyses will have more than one test of significance relevant to our hypothesis and, since for every test of significance there is an effect size estimate, these studies will have more than one effect size estimate as well. The various dependent variables employed in a study should all be examined for clues as to the types of dependent variable that seem most affected and least affected by the independent variable of interest. If there are many studies using several of the same dependent variables one could perform a separate meta-analysis for each different type of dependent variable involved. For example, if one were studying the effects of alcoholism treatment programs, separate analyses could be performed for the dependent variables of sobriety, number of days of employment, number of arrests, general medical health, personal and social adjustment, and so on. Each of these types of dependent variable could be operationalized in several ways. For example, for each of them we could obtain self-reports, family reports, and institutional reports (e.g., from hospitals, clinics, courts, police departments, etc.).

Table 2.6 shows a matrix of 6 types of dependent variables crossed by 3 sources of information. If there were a set of studies that had employed all of the $6 \times 3 = 18$ specific dependent variables, we could perform a separate meta-analysis on each of the 6 types of variables averaged across all 3 sources of information to learn which variable, on the average, was most affected by the treatment. We could also perform a separate meta-analysis on each of the three sources of information averaged across all 6 types of

TABLE 2.6
Matrix of Hypothetical Dependent Variables Obtained in a
Set of Studies of Alcoholism Treatment Programs

Type of Variable	Source of Information			Mean
	Self-Report	Family Report	Institutional Report	
Days of sobriety				
Days of employment				
Number of arrests				
Medical health				
Personal adjustment				
Social adjustment				
Mean				

variables to learn which of the sources was most affected by the treatment. We could examine these matters simultaneously for a set of K studies by entering effect sizes (or Z's associated with significance levels) into each of the $6 \times 3 = 18$ cells of the matrix and then conducting a $K \times 6 \times 3$ analysis of variance on the effect sizes (or the Z's). In such an analysis there would be K independent sampling units (studies) and repeated measures on the 6 level factor of variable type and on the 3 level factor of information source. Such an analysis would be of great value for the simultaneous light it might shed on the effects of variable type, information source, and the interaction of these variables on the magnitude of the experimental effects obtained.

Unfortunately, we do not often encounter such nicely filled-in matrices of effect sizes. Indeed, we count ourselves fortunate when even a substantial subset of studies have employed the same types of variables. Assuming the typical situation, then, how are we to analyze multiple results from a single study? Shall we count each result from a different dependent variable as though it were a separate study, i.e., as though it were an independent result? Smith et al. (1980) and Glass et al. (1981) have treated multiple results as though they were independent. For the very large numbers of studies they have had available, this procedure may turn out to be fairly accurate in the estimation of average effect sizes. However, because we cannot be sure of this and because the various methods of combining probability levels require independent research results, we recommend that in the final overall analysis each sample of subjects or other units normally contribute only a single effect size and a single significance level to the total.

In the following sections some procedures are proposed that can be used to obtain a single research result from a set of correlated research results. We begin by describing procedures applicable in the usual meta-analytic situation in which we are given relatively few details in the report available to us. Subsequently we describe procedures applicable when more of the original data are available to us.

In most of these applications we will find that significance levels and effect sizes are highly correlated. That follows from the fact that most correlated results will be based on approximately the same sample size. When that is the case there tends to be a perfect monotonic relationship between significance level and effect size.

IV.A. Solutions When Original Data Are Not Available

IV.A.1. Method of mean result. Perhaps the most obvious method of obtaining a single result for a set of results from a single study is to calculate the mean level of significance and the mean effect size. Suppose we have a set of three one-tailed p levels: .25, .10, and .001. To average these p's we first find the standard normal deviate (Z) corresponding to each, and average these Z's. (If results are simply reported as nonsignificant, and we have no further information available, we have no choice but to assume a p level of .50, or a Z of 0.00.) In this example, our three Z's are .67, 1.28, and 3.09. All three Z's have positive signs because all results were in the same direction. The mean of our three Z's is [.67 + 1.28 + 3.09]/3 = 5.04/3 = 1.68, a Z corresponding to a p of .046. It should be emphasized that when we average p levels it is their associated Z's we average and not the p levels themselves. This is discussed in detail in Chapters 4 and 5.

To average several effect size estimates we simply take their mean if they are already in standard deviation units as in Cohen's d, Glass's Δ, and Hedges's g. In the case of r, we first transform each r value to z_r before finding the mean. If effect sizes have not been given we can compute our own, one for each p level, as long as we know N, the number of sampling units, since

$$r = \frac{Z}{\sqrt{N}}$$
[2.18]

For the preceding three p levels we would find corresponding r's of .067, .128, and .309 if N = 100. The z_r's associated with these r's are found to be .07, .13, and .32, yielding a mean z_r of .17 corresponding to an r of .17. When r's are all quite low, averaging directly yields results essentially like those obtained when we first transform the r's to z_r's. For the present example, direct averaging of r's also yields a mean r of .17.

An alternative procedure is to compute the mean p level and then simply compute the effect size corresponding to it. Although the two estimates will often yield similar values, it should be noted that the mean of a set of effect sizes, each based on an associated p, is a *different* statistic than is the effect size associated with the mean p level. For example, imagine two p levels from the same study (N = 100) associated with standard normal deviates of 0.00 and 9.00. Their mean is a Z of 4.5. The effect size r associated with this mean Z is

$$r = \frac{4.5}{\sqrt{100}} = .45$$

However, the two effect sizes associated with Z's of 0.00 and 9.00 are r's of .00 and .90 but z_r's of 0.00 and 1.47, respectively. The mean of these z_r's is about .74 corresponding to an r of .63. Clearly the two methods can yield quite different results (.63 versus .45), neither of which is intrinsically more correct than the other. A reasonable practice is to decide beforehand on one of these procedures and use it throughout any given meta-analysis. In no case, however, should both procedures be employed unless both are reported. In other words, it will not do to compute both estimates and then report or use in the meta-analysis only the personally preferred estimate.

Sometimes only one or two p levels are reported when a whole array of effect sizes is available. That might happen, for example, if the report provides a correlation matrix in which the dummy-coded (0,1) independent variable is correlated with a whole series of dependent variables. In this case, of course, we would base our effect size estimate on the mean of all the effect sizes, not just those for which p levels are reported. In addition, we base our p level estimate on the mean of all the p levels associated with all the effect sizes reported. By rearrangement from equation 2.18 we can get the Z associated with each p from the following:

$$Z = r\sqrt{N}$$

An alternative to computing the mean of all the Z's obtained from this procedure is to compute only the Z associated with the mean effect size. The cautions given above about the process of choosing one of these procedures to present as "the result" should be kept in mind.

IV.A.2. Method of median result. When the p levels and/or the effect sizes produced by a single study are very skewed, some meta-analysts may prefer to compute the median p level and the median effect size. Although there are a great many statistical applications where medians are to be preferred to means (Tukey, 1977), the use of medians in meta-analytic work tends to give results consistently favoring type II errors, i.e., results leading to estimates favoring the null hypothesis. An intuitively clear example might be the following five p levels, all one-tailed: .25, .18, .16, .001, and .00003. The median p of .16 is notably larger than the mean p of .027 associated with the mean Z of 1.93. Intuition may suggest that the mean is a better estimate of the gist of the five p levels than is the median, given two such very significant results in the set of five correlated results. That intuition will be supported by the logic of the Bonferroni-based methods to be discussed next.

IV.A.3. Method of ensemble-adjustment of p. Suppose we had four p levels for a given study: .50, .50, .50. and .001. The median p is .50 and the mean p is .22. But somehow we think that, of four results, we should not find a p as low as .001 if the null hypothesis were true. The Bonferroni-based procedures address such issues. One can examine a set of R correlated results for a single study, compute the most significant p, and calculate the conservative corrected p that this most significant found p could have been obtained, after examining R results, if the null hypothesis were true (Rosenthal & Rubin, 1983). All that needs to be done is to multiply the most significant p (p_{ms}) by R, the number of p levels that were examined to find the most significant p. Thus, for our example of R = 4 p levels where the most significant p was .001, the ensemble-adjusted p value is

$$p \text{ adjusted} = (R) \ p_{ms} = (4).001 = .004 \qquad [2.29]$$

This procedure for correlated results, which is related to Tippett's (1931) procedure applied to independent samples, is employed when we have no theoretical reasons to expect certain results to be more significant than others. When we have theoretical reasons to expect some results to be more significant than others, we can increase our power by assigning weights to each of the results to correspond to our view of their importance. (The actual assignment of weights must be done by an investigator blind to the results obtained.) For example, suppose we knew a study to yield four p levels. Before examining the results we decided that the first result was of greatest importance with weight 5, the second and third results were of less importance with weights of 2 each, and the fourth result was of least importance with weight 1. Suppose we obtained one-tailed p's of .02, .19, .24, and .40, respectively. Then the weighted adjusted p level for the most significant result would be given by

$$p \text{ adjusted, weighted} = \left(\frac{\sum \text{weights}}{\text{weight of } p_{ms}} \right) p_{ms}$$

$$= \left(\frac{5 + 2 + 2 + 1}{5} \right) .02 = .04 \qquad [2.30]$$

Therefore, the adjusted, weighted p is significant at p < .05, whereas the unweighted adjusted p value would not have been, since

$$p \text{ adjusted} = (R) p_{ms} = (4).02 = .08.$$

In addition, the mean p would have been .17, and the median p would have been .21. Further details on assigning weights in Bonferroni-based procedures are given in Rosenthal and Rubin (in press). Once we have computed our ensemble-adjusted p we compute the associated effect size from equation 2.18.

IV.B. Solutions When Original Data Are Available

IV.B.1. Creating a single supervariable. When we have access to the original data, an examination of the intercorrelations of our dependent variables may suggest that all our dependent variables are substantially intercorrelated. If that is the case we may want to create a supervariable made up of all our dependent variables. One easy way to do so is to standard-score (z score) each of our dependent variables and form the supervariable as the mean of the z scores earned on the contributing variables. This procedure weights the variables equally. If we have a priori theoretical reasons for weighting some variables more heavily than others we can do so. Any variable in its z score transformation can be multiplied by any weight w_i we like. Any subject's score on the supervariable z_w is then defined by the sum of that subject's z scores, each multiplied by its weight, and this sum divided by the sum of all the weights employed, or

$$\bar{z}_w = \frac{\sum (w_i z_i)}{\sum w_i} \qquad [2.31]$$

where $\bar{z}_w$ is the mean weighted z score or supervariable score for any one subject, and w_i is the weight given to the ith z score (z_i).

As an example, imagine a subject whose z scores on four dependent variables are 1.10, .66, 1.28, and .92. The weights (w_i) assigned to each of these variables were decided on a priori theoretical grounds to be 4, 2, 1, and 1, respectively. Therefore, employing equation 2.31, our subject's supervariable score ($\bar{z}_w$) would be:

$$\bar{z}_w = \frac{\sum (w_i z_i)}{\sum w_i} = \frac{(4)1.10 + (2).66 + (1)1.28 + (1).92}{4 + 2 + 1 + 1} = \frac{7.92}{8} = .99$$

If we want an estimate of the internal consistency reliability of the supervariable, we can obtain it by one of three ways: (1) applying the Spearman-

Brown formula to the mean of the intercorrelations among the constituent variables, (2) computing an intraclass correlation following an analysis of variance in which constituent variables become a repeated measures factor, or (3) computing Armor's theta from the unrotated first principal component. All three of these procedures are described in some detail in the following chapter and are summarized elsewhere (Rosenthal, 1982a).

An alternative to combining variables by z scoring is to combine the raw scores. This is a reasonable alternative only when the standard deviations of each of the constituent variables are similar. If they are not, the variables with larger variances dominate the others in the supervariable, usually for no good theoretical reason. For example, one variable, ability test score, may have $\sigma = 20$ while another variable, acceptance into a particular college (scored as 1 or 0) may have $\sigma = 0.50$. Adding raw scores from these variables would yield a new variable that was very little affected by the second variable (acceptance).

Situations in which direct adding of variables often is useful include those in which the variables are ratings by others on a specific rating scale, scores on subtests of personality tests of cognitive functioning. In no case, however, should variables in raw score form be combined without an examination of the standard deviations of the variables. If the ratio of the largest to the smallest σ is 1.5 or less, combining is safe. A larger ratio than 1.5 may be tolerated when the number of variables to be combined grows larger.

IV.B.2. Creating uncorrelated variables. A procedure that seems not to have been used in meta-analytic work, but which may hold some promise, involves a principal components (factor) analysis of the set of dependent variables. A principal components analysis takes a set of V variables and transforms them into a new set of V variables (called components) that are uncorrelated with each other (Rosenthal & Rosnow, 1984a). The first component accounts for more of the common variance than does the second, the second accounts for more than the third, and so on. All of the information in the original variables has been preserved in the components, but, since the components are independent of each other (while the original variables were not), we can employ the techniques of combining independent results on the set of independent components.

Rather than weighting all the components equally, we may want to weight them by the proportion of the total variance that each accounts for, or equivalently, by their eigenvalues. Instead of, or in addition to, weighting by their eigenvalues, we may want to weight the components by their substantive meaningfulness. This latter weighting must be done *before* the components are employed as dependent variables so that we will not be tempted to call more meaningful those components that are affected by the independent variable as our theoretical position might require.

The computational procedures for combining and comparing independent results are described in a later chapter, but for now a cautionary note about size of study should be entered. Since we now have V independent assessments of our N subjects, the overall combined p level will be based on a new study size of V × N. Therefore, if we compute our effect size estimate from the combined p level we should use the following equation to obtain r:

$$r \text{ combined} = \frac{Z \text{ combined}}{\sqrt{VN}}$$

[2.32]

where r combined is the effect size corresponding to the combined p, Z combined is the Z associated with the combined p, V is the number of principal components combined, and N is the number of subjects or other sampling units in the study. If we forget that, by making our variables independent of each other, we have increased our df or our N, we will get an estimate of the effect size that will be too large—often far too large.

V. A SUMMARY OF SOME EFFECT SIZE INDICATORS

In this section we want to bring together the various effect size indicators that have been referred to as well as a few others that may prove useful. Table 2.7 serves as a summary. The first four indicators include the very general Pearson product moment correlation (r) and three related indices. The indicator r/k is not typically employed as an effect size estimate though it certainly could be. It is included here because of its role in equations 2.3 and 2.11; that is, it is an effect size estimate that needs only to be multiplied by $\sqrt{df}$ to yield the associated test of significance, t. The index r/k turns out also to be related to Cohen's d in an interesting way—it equals d/2 for situations in which we can think of the two populations being compared as equally numerous (Cohen, 1977; Friedman, 1968). The indicator z_r is also not typically employed as an effect size estimate though it, too, could be. However, it is frequently used as a transformation of r in a variety of meta-analytic procedures. Cohen's q indexes the difference between two correlation coefficients in units of z_r.

The next three indicators of Table 2.7 are all standardized mean differences. They differ from each other only in the standardizing denominator. Cohen's d employs the σ computed from both groups employing N rather than N−1 as the within group divisor for the sums of squares. Glass's Δ and

TABLE 2.7
Three Types of Effect Size Indicators

	Effect Size Indicator	*Definition*
Product Moment Correlation (r) and Functions of r	Pearson r	$\Sigma(z_x z_y)/N$
	r/k	$r/\sqrt{1-r^2}$
	z_r	$\frac{1}{2} \log_e \left[\frac{1+r}{1-r} \right]$
	Cohen's q	$z_{r_1} - z_{r_2}$[a]
Standardized Differences Between Means	Cohen's d	$(M_1 - M_2)/\sigma$ pooled
	Glass's Δ	$(M_1 - M_2)/S$ control group
	Hedges's g	$(M_1 - M_2)/S$ pooled
Differences Between Proportions	Cohen's g	$P - .50$
	d'	$P_1 - P_2$
	Cohen's h	$P_1^b - P_2^b$

a. This is an effect size indexing the magnitude of the difference between two effect sizes.
b. P's are first transformed to angles measured in radians: $2 \arcsin \sqrt{P}$.

Hedges's g both employ $N-1$ divisors for sums of squares. Glass, however, computes S only for the control group, while Hedges computes S from both experimental and control groups.

The last three indicators of Table 2.7 include two from Cohen (1977). Cohen's g is the difference between an obtained proportion and a proportion of .50. The index d' is the difference between two obtained proportions. Cohen's h is also the difference between two obtained proportions but only after the proportions have been transformed to angles (measured in units called radians, equal to about 57.3 degrees).

Many other effect size indicators could have been listed. For example, Kraemer and Andrews (1982) and Krauth (1983) have described effect size estimates when medians rather than means are to be compared. These are not described here since the product moment correlations (based on continuous scores, ranks, or dichotomized data) can be employed in those situations. We have specifically not included any indices of proportion of variance accounted for such as r^2, eta^2, omega^2, epsilon^2, and so on. As we shall see in the final chapter, all these indices tend to be misleading at the lower levels. In addition, those that are based on F tests with df > 1 in the numerator are generally of little use in the meta-analytic enterprise.

3

Retrieving and Assessing Research Results

Procedures for locating and abstracting research results are described and illustrated, and the reliability of these procedures is discussed. Various types of errors, their prevention and correction are described. Finally, the evaluation of the quality of research results is discussed.

There is in principle no difference between the conscientious review of a research area conducted traditionally or meta-analytically. In both cases one wants to find all the research results. There may be logistic and financial reasons for restricting a review simply to published works, but there are no scholarly reasons for doing so if our goal is to summarize the research evidence bearing on a given relationship. After we have retrieved all the retrievable research results, we will want to evaluate whether the sources of our results are significantly and substantially related to the quality of the research conducted and the magnitude of the effects obtained. If they are, we can present our meta-analytic results separately for the various sources of information and the various levels of quality of the research conducted.

I. RETRIEVING RESEARCH RESULTS

I.A. Locating Research Results

Locating research results has become a more sophisticated enterprise than spending a few hours with the *Psychological Abstracts, Sociological Abstracts, Child Development Abstracts, Language and Language Behavior Abstracts,* or the *International Bibliography of Social and Cultural Anthropology.* Computer-based retrieval systems are not only available but are being enlarged and improved at a rate so rapid that few social scientists can be truly expert in the methods of information retrieval. That is the domain of the information specialist. To give the details required for the serious retrieval of the results of a research area there is a useful paper on information retrieval especially prepared for meta-anlaysts by an experienced reference librarian (M. Rosenthal, 1984).

When the resources described in that paper have been properly employed, including an examination of the references of the retrieved documents and correspondence with the contributors to a research area to obtain their unpublished manuscripts and their suggestions as to the location of other unpublished works, we will find four major classes of documents: (1) Books, including authored books, edited books, and chapters in edited books; (2) Journals, including professional journals, published newsletters, magazines, and newspapers; (3) Theses, including doctoral, master's, and bachelor's theses; (4) Unpublished work, including technical reports, grant proposals, grant reports, convention papers not published in proceedings, ERIC reports, films, cassette recordings, and other unpublished materials.

I.A.1. Reliability of information sources. The purpose of this section is to present the results of a new analysis showing that, for a sample of meta-analyses, there is a high degree of reliability among the four types of documents in the average effect size obtained. The raw data for these analyses comes from Glass et al. (1981, pp. 66-67). The results of 12 meta-analyses on various topics are presented. For each meta-analysis, an effect size (Glass's Δ or Cohen's d) was estimated from at least two different information sources.

Table 3.1 shows the six possible pairs of sources of information, the number of meta-analyses providing effect size estimates for each pair of sources, the reliability obtained between the two sources of each pair, (computed over all available areas meta-analyzed) and the p level of the reliabil-

TABLE 3.1
Reliability of Information Sources
for a Sample of Meta-Analyses

Pairs of Sources	Number (n) of Meta-Analyses	Reliability (r) of Sources	p Level of Reliability
Journal; thesis	10	.89	.0005
Journal; unpublished	7	.65	.06
Thesis; unpublished	7	.85	.008
Book; journal	6	.82	.025
Book; thesis	4	.96	.02
Book; unpublished	3	1.00	.005
Median	6.5	.87	.014
Weighted Median	7	.85	.008
Weighted (n − 2) Mean		.83	

ity obtained. The median (unweighted and weighted) reliabilities of .87 and .85 and the weighted mean r of .83 show that there is a high degree of reliability, on the average, between the various pairs of information sources. There is little support here for the position that holds that some sources of information may be misleading relative to the others. On the basis of the 12 meta-analyses available, we can conclude that meta-analyses finding larger effect sizes from one source of information are also likely to find larger effect sizes from other sources of information.

I.A.2. Differences among information sources. High reliability of sources of information does not necessarily mean that sources will agree in their estimates of effect sizes for a given meta-analytic review. Two sources could have perfect reliability ($r = 1.00$) yet differ greatly in the effect sizes estimated, so long as the difference was constant for every meta-analysis. The purpose of this section is to present the results of a new analysis investigating systematic differences among information sources in the average effect size found. Our raw data again come from Glass et al. (1981, pp. 66-67).

For each of the 12 meta-analyses, the mean effect sizes are reported for all those sources that provided relevant information. If there had been four sources of information available for each of the 12 meta-analyses, we would have been able to provide a simpler answer to our question by merely examining the means or medians obtained from all four sources. Unfortunately, only 3 of the 12 meta-analyses provided data from all four sources; 13 of the possible 48 (12×4) estimates were not available. Under these conditions, comparing the grand means or medians of each of the sources of information confounds the source of information with the area being summarized.

As a rough guide to the likelihood that such confounding might be a problem, Table 3.2 was prepared. It shows the median effect size obtained from journal information for those meta-analyses in which the other sources of information were or were not available. Thus the median effect size of meta-analyses in which books were not available was .64 but the median effect size was only .44 when books were available. It appears, then, that we might erroneously conclude that books underestimate effect sizes relative to journals when actually it just happened that books were available as an information source for those areas of research showing smaller effect sizes anyway (as defined by journal information).

Table 3.2 shows that the availability of unpublished material was unrelated to effect sizes estimated from journal sources. This suggests no problem of biased availability of studies as there had been for books as sources of information. The result for thesis-based information showed a small tendency for meta-analyses for which theses were available to be associated with somewhat larger effect sizes (as defined by journal information). The data base is not large enough to warrant firm conclusions, but the data are

TABLE 3.2
Median Effect Sizes Obtained from Journal Information
for Meta-Analyses in Which Other Sources
Were or Were Not Available

Information Source	Source Available	Source Unavailable	Mean Difference	Mean
Book	.44[6]a	.64[6]	−.20	.54
Thesis	.51[10]	.40[2]	.11	.46
Unpublished	.50[7]	.49[5]	.01	.50
Mean	.48	.51	−.03	.50[b]

a. The number of meta-analyses on which the median is based is shown in parentheses.
b. The median of all 12 meta-analyses based on journal information alone was also .50.

TABLE 3.3
Pairwise Comparisons of Effect Sizes Obtained
from Four Information Sources

Pairs of Sources	Number (n) of Meta-Analyses	First Mean Δa	Second Mean Δa	Mean Difference	Median Difference
Journal; thesis	10	.56	.30	.26[b]	.22
Journal; unpublished	7	.56	.64	−.08	.05
Thesis; unpublished	7	.31	.64	−.33	−.07
Book; journal	6	.34	.42	−.08	.00
Book; thesis	4	.40	.27	.13	.14
Book; unpublished	3	.31	.68	−.37	−.09

a. Note that our purpose is not to estimate the average effect size obtained from specific sources of information since that depends most heavily on the areas meta-analyzed. Our purpose is to estimate as well as we can the difference between average sizes obtained from various sources of information.
b. This is the only significant mean difference t(9) = 4.78, p = .001, two-tailed (p = .001 by sign test as well).

suggestive enough that we should try to assess differences among information sources correcting for sampling bias. This type of correction can be achieved by considering each type of source pairwise with every other source as shown in Table 3.3.

The first and second columns of Table 3.3 show the two paired sources of information and the number of meta-analyses upon which each pairwise comparison is based. The third and fourth columns give the mean effect size (Δ) found for the first and second named source, respectively. The fifth column gives the difference between the means with the second subtracted from the first. The final column, and perhaps the most important, gives the median of the n difference scores for each set of matched pairs. The only significant mean difference shows larger effect sizes obtained from journals than from theses (excess of $\Delta = .26$ and $.22$ for mean and median differences, respectively). These results support the conclusion drawn by Glass et al. (1981) though the present pairwise analysis, controlling for the confounding of topic and source, shows a difference larger by between 37% and 63% than that reported by Glass et al.

There is certainly no clear difference between mean effect sizes obtained from journals compared to unpublished materials. The mean difference favors one by $.08\ \Delta$ units; the median difference favors the other by $.05\ \Delta$ units. The results of this analysis very strongly suggest that the burden of proof now rests on those who claim that unpublished (not unretrieved but retrievable unpublished) studies are biased in their results relative to published studies.

On the average, theses obtain smaller effect sizes than do unpublished studies but the difference shrinks dramatically when the median difference is employed rather than the mean difference.

Books and journals tend to obtain very similar effect sizes but books do tend to obtain somewhat higher effect sizes than do theses. Finally, books tend to obtain smaller effect sizes than do unpublished papers but the median difference is not large and, given the small n (3), even the large mean difference of .37 could be a sampling fluctuation ($p = .45$).

There is no simple way to summarize the data of Table 3.3. One provisional method that preserves the pairwise nature of the comparisons is to consider in turn all pairwise comparisons of each of the four sources with all others and report the median of all these comparisons. Table 3.4 shows that journal articles, unpublished manuscripts, and books are essentially indistinguishable from each other. However, theses tend to yield noticeably smaller effect sizes than do the other three sources of information— smaller, that is, by about 1/5 of a standard deviation.

How might we explain this bias for theses to yield smaller effect sizes? One analysis that may be instructive was carried out as part of a meta-analysis by Rosenthal and Rubin (1978). In their study of 345 studies of interpersonal ex-

TABLE 3.4
Pairwise Comparisons of Effect Sizes Obtained
From Each Source Against All Others

Source	Number of Pairwise Comparisons	Median Difference
Journal	23	.13
Unpublished	17	.07
Book	13	.07
Thesis	21	$-.20$
Absolute median	19	.10

TABLE 3.5
Mean Effect Sizes (d) for Dissertation and Nondissertation Studies
Employing or Not Employing Special Control Procedures

	Dissertations	Nondissertations	Unweighted Mean	Weighted Mean
Special controls	.78[18]a	.54[25]	.66	.64
No special controls	−.09[14]	.75[288]	.33	.71
Unweighted mean	.345	.645	.495	
Weighted mean	.40	.73		.70

a. The number of studies on which the mean is based is shown in parentheses.

pectancy effects, they computed separate analyses for dissertation and non-dissertation studies and found that dissertations did indeed yield substantially smaller effects on the average. Each of the 345 studies in their sample was also classified by whether the investigator(s) had taken special pains to control for errors of recording or cheating by the experimenters or teachers being studied.

Table 3.5 shows the mean effect sizes obtained in dissertations and non-dissertations that either had or had not instituted special controls for intentional or unintentional errors. Most of the variation (93%) among the four estimated mean effect sizes was due to the difference between dissertations employing no special controls and the remaining three groups of studies which differed relatively little among themselves. These results suggest the possibility that the tendency for theses to yield smaller effect sizes than other sources of information may be due primarily to the less carefully executed of the theses.

Before leaving the comparison of theses with other information sources, we should note that theses were conspicuously over-represented among the studies instituting special controls for intentional or unintentional errors. The correlation between being a thesis and employing special controls was .42 ($\chi^2(1) = 62.0$, N = 345, p < .0001). Of the nondissertations, only 8% employed special controls; of the dissertations, however, 56% did so. The typical dissertation, then, may be more carefully done than the typical non-dissertation. Perhaps this is due to the healthy monitoring that is often carried out by a conscientious dissertation committee.

I.B. Abstracting Research Results

Once we have located the studies to include in our meta-analysis, we must decide what information is to be abstracted from each document. We know from the last chapter that we will always want to record both the significance level and the size of the effect and that, if one of these is not provided, we can estimate it if we know the size of the study. But what else are we to record for each study? The answer, of course, depends on the specific goals of our meta-analysis. It is easiest to begin with examples of useful formats for abstracting information from studies.

I.B.1. Interpersonal expectancy effects. Since the early 1960s the present writer has been conducting meta-analyses of studies of the effects of experimenters' (or teachers' or clinicians') expectations on the response obtained from their subjects (or pupils, or patients). For each of the studies retrieved, the following information was typically recorded:

(1) *Complete reference,* as for a bibliography.
(2) *Authors' full names and addresses,* so that they could be contacted for further information about the study in question, about their work in progress, and about the work of others in the same general area.
(3) *Sex of data collector,* since the sex of data collector may be related to the results obtained.
(4) *Status of data collector,* e.g., faculty member, doctoral candidate, graduate student, undergraduate, and so on, since it has been found that the status of the data collector may affect the results obtained.
(5) *Relationship of data collector to meta-analyst,* so that correlations could be computed between the results obtained and the degree of acquaintanceship with the meta-analyst (Rosenthal, 1969).
(6) *Sex of subjects,* number of each sex who served as subjects, pupils, or patients.
(7) *Nature of subject sample,* i.e., where and how obtained.
(8) *Sex of experimenters,* number of each sex who served as experimenters, teachers, or clinicians.
(9) *Nature of experimenter sample,* i.e., where and how obtained.
(10) *Relative status of experimenters,* since smaller expectancy effects are obtained when there is little status differential favoring the experimenter.
(11) *Task, test, or other behavior of subjects* constituting the dependent variable.
(12) *Unusual design features,* e.g., not an experiment but causal inference strengthened by use of such procedures as cross-lagged panel analysis, analysis of covariance, partial correlations, path analysis, and so forth.
(13) *Additional control groups,* as when high and low induced-expectancy conditions can be compared to a randomly assigned group of no-induced-expectancy subjects.
(14) *Procedural controls for cheating and/or observer error,* as when all interactions are filmed, videotaped, or otherwise monitored, and/ or when experimenters' recordings can be otherwise checked.

(15) *Moderating variables,* variables associated with differences in obtained results, the direction of their effect, effect size, and significance level.

(16) *Mediation data,* any results bearing on the processes by which experimenters, teachers, or clinicians may have communicated their expectations to their subjects, pupils, or patients.

(17) *Expectancy effect,* effect size (including direction) and significance level associated with the effects of the experimenters', teachers', or clinicians' expectancies.

I.B.2. Psychotherapy outcome. A more detailed type of abstracting was employed by Glass and his colleagues (e.g., et al., 1981, pp. 80–91, 233–237) in their seminal meta-analysis of psychotherapy outcome experiments. They divided their coding into the methodological and substantive features that are briefly summarized here:

I.B.2.a. Methodological features. These included (1) date of publication, (2) type of publication, (3) degree to which experimenter was blind, (4) how clients were obtained, (5) how clients were assigned to conditions, (6) client loss for each condition, (7) internal validity, (8) experimenter's probable preference for outcomes, and (9) reactivity of outcome measure.

I.B.2.b. Substantive features. These included: (10) professional field of experimenter, (11) similarity of client to therapist, (12) diagnosis of client, (13) duration of previous hospitalization, (14) intelligence of typical client, (15) mode of therapy (e.g., individual, group), (16) site of therapy, (17) duration of therapy, (18) therapist experience or status level, (19) outcome measures, (20) type of psychotherapy, (21) degree of confidence in deciding type of therapy, and (22) effect size.

I.B.3. Ethnic group and social class differences in need for achievement. A very focused type of abstracting was employed by Harris Cooper (1984) in his comparison of ethnic groups and social class levels on need for achievement. A summary of his coding sheet follows: (1) complete citation; (2) source of reference; (3) sex of subjects, with n of each, for the two groups being compared; (4) average age of subjects in each group; (5) geographic location of each group; (6) other restrictions pertaining to each group; (7) ethnicity of each group; (8) mean and S of each ethnic group on need for achievement; (9) type of significance test and df error employed; (10) value of test statistic obtained, and df effect; (11) p level and effect size obtained; (12) direction of results; (13) social class of each group; (14) standardized vs. informal measure of social class for each group; (15) basis of classification for each group including occupation, salary, social status, or other; (16) mean and S of each social class group on need for achievement; (17-20) items 9-12 (above) repeated for social class comparison; (21) dependent measures including TAT (n-Ach), French's Test of Insight, California Psychological Inventory, or other; and (22) variables interacting with ethnicity or social class.

I.B.4. Constructing a format for abstracting research results. Examination of the preceding three examples of abstracting formats will be useful in the construction of a new format. Using these examples and a process of free association, the beginning meta-analyst can construct a preliminary form. This form should then be discussed with colleagues and advisors who can suggest other variables to be included. Finally, a revised form might be sent to workers in the area of the meta-analysis, with an invitation to have them suggest other variables that should be coded.

I.C. The Reliability of Retrieval

I.C.1. Reliability of locating research results. It would be useful to know the reliability of locating research results. If two meta-analysts set out to retrieve the relevant research results for the same research question, how closely would their acquisitions agree? No empirical answer to that question is available. We do know that if each meta-analyst employed only one (or two) research indices, each would miss an appreciable proportion of retrievable studies (Glass et al., 1981, pp. 63-65). A thorough retrieval effort, however, would involve going well beyond one or two research indices (M. Rosenthal, 1984).

It is not even obvious how one would determine the correlation defining reliability in the situation of our two meta-analysts. Would we set up a 2×2 table with columns representing the first meta-analyst's choices (i.e., included vs. not included in the analysis), and with rows representing the second meta-analyst's choices (i.e., included vs. not included in the analysis)? What would be the entry for the cell included in neither analysis? Would it be the hundreds of thousands of studies not relevant to the analysis? Whatever the problem of computing (or even defining) the reliability of locating research results, the problems are identical whether the research summarizing process is to be traditional or meta-analytic.

I.C.2. Reliability of coding study features. When we try to estimate the reliability of the coding of studies after they have been retrieved, we can do quite a bit better. Several studies have reported proportions of agreement on specific items as coded by two judges.

Table 3.6 presents a summary of two of these studies. Study 1 is by Stock, Okun, Haring, Miller, Kinney, and Ceurvorst (1982), and Study 2 is by Jackson (1978). For each study sample items are given to illustrate items associated with varying proportions of agreement from below .50 to 1.00.

TABLE 3.6
Examples of Items Obtaining Various
Proportions of Agreement

Proportion of Agreement	Study 1	Study 2
1.00	Median age	Name of periodical
.96-.99	Mean age	Research index used?
.92-.95	Age range	Own studies cited?
.88-.91	Total N	Secondary analyses done?
.84-.87	Was median age reported?	Specific recommendations?
.80-.83	Type of bivariate relationship	Relationship exists?
.70-.79	Type of sampling procedure	Critique of prior reviews?
.60-.69	—	Percentage of studies cited that are not directly relevant
.50-.59	Total number of subsamples	Percentage of studies examining interaction effect
.40-.49	—	Are surveys among the major approaches employed?
Number of items	25	65
Range	.57-1.00	.44-1.00
25th to 75th percentile	.86-.965	.71-.87
Median	.92	.79

Median proportions of agreement are very substantial but we could have had more confidence in the interpretation of these data had the correlations been provided rather than the proportion of agreements. It is possible to have near perfect agreement and still have reliability coefficients of only about .50. More detailed discussion of this problem is available in Lewin and Wakefield (1979), Rosenthal (1982a), Wakefield (1980), and in our subsequent discussion of effective reliability, especially the final paragraph on product moment correlations (section II.C.1.a. of this chapter).

I.C.3. Reliability of significance level and effect size estimates. Perhaps the two things we want to code most reliably are the results themselves: results defined as significance levels and effect size estimates. Unfortunately there appear to be no reliability data on the estimation of significance levels as such. We come close in the raw data of the study by Cooper and Rosenthal (1980) described earlier. As part of that study, 19 meta-analysts were asked to decide whether a given set of seven studies supported the rejection of the null hypothesis. From the analysis of variance of the 19×7 data matrix, we were able to compute the intraclass correlation which is analogous to the average interjudge reliability. For the 19 meta-analysts, this correlation was .969, a very high degree of reliability. In a situation where accurate p levels were being estimated (rather than accept-reject decisions) and meta-analysts might not even have retrieved the same studies, and different procedures for combining p levels might have been used, the reliability would surely be lower.

When we turn to the estimation of effect sizes, relevant data are provided by Glass et al. (1981). They had six studies for each of which two judges computed Glass's Δ as the effect size estimate. The mean absolute difference between the pairs of judges was only .07 standard deviation units (Δ's). The mean algebraic difference was even smaller—.01 standard deviation units! Reliability, however, is indexed by a correlation coefficient rather than a mean difference and it is possible in principle to have a very small mean difference (i.e., excellent agreement in mean judgments) yet have a low reliability. That did not occur in this case. For the set of six studies and two judgments per study, the intraclass correlation was .993.

Should future studies yield lower reliabilities, Glass et al. would not be surprised nor would I. As the former authors point out, although the definition of Δ (and of other effect size estimates) is simple, in actual practice judgments must be made, assumptions must be made, and series of calculations must be made and all of these may be made somewhat differently by equally well-trained and experienced meta-analysts.

II. ASSESSING RESEARCH RESULTS

II.A. Correcting Research Results

The purpose of this section is to emphasize that error-making is normal. The meta-analyst will make mistakes and the authors of the studies summarized will have made mistakes. Careful reading of the original papers by the meta-analyst will often reveal errors. Fortunately, these errors can often be corrected before the meta-analytic procedures are applied (Rosenthal & Rubin, 1978).

One type of error that is difficult for the meta-analyst to correct or even to diagnose is an error of recording the data as the data were being obtained by the original investigator. How often do recording errors occur? When they do occur, are they likely to favor the investigator's research hypothesis? Building on some earlier work on this topic (Rosenthal, 1978b), I was able to collect 27 studies for this book that yielded some up-to-date information on these two questions. Since most of these studies were designed at least in part to permit the quantitative assessment of error rates, they can not be regarded as representative of behavioral research in general. We have no way of knowing, however, whether these studies are likely to yield overestimates or underestimates of rates of error-making. The 27 studies ranged widely in terms of research area and locus of data collection, e.g., studies of reaction time, person perception, learning (human and animal), task ability, psychophysical judgments, questionnaire responses, classroom behavior, and mental telepathy. In addition to behavioral research, legal research and health research were represented. Although there were not enough studies in these various categories to permit sensitive comparisons, there appeared to be no clear relationship between area of research and either the rate of recording errors or the likelihood of errors being biased when they did occur.

In most of the studies, errors were defined only in terms of misrecording a response that was either seen or heard by the data recorder. In a few cases, however, simple arithmetic was also required by the recorder so that observer errors could not be distinguished from arithmetic errors. In these cases, however, the results were so close to the results of studies of simple recording errors that they could safely be grouped together, at least for our present purpose.

It is also important that for almost all the 27 studies located, the observers had finished their task to their satisfaction and did not know that their observations would be checked for errors. Thus whatever checking could be done or was going to be done by the observers had been done at the time of the analysis of errors. It is unlikely, therefore, that the estimates of error were inflated due to the observers' not having finished their checking operations.

Not all of the studies provided the data in directly usable form and it was necessary to make some estimates from data provided. For example, an investigator might mention in passing that 10 responses were misrecorded by the observers but not how many observations were recorded altogether. A reasonable estimate of this total was often available, however, as when the investigator reported that 5 observers each collected data from 10 participants each of whom made 20 responses (e.g., $5 \times 10 \times 20 = 1000$).

Table 3.7 shows, for each of the 27 studies, the number of observers involved, the number of recordings made, the number of errors committed, the percentage of all recordings that were wrong, and the percentage of the errors committed that favored the hypothesis of the observer. Tables 3.8 and 3.9 present stem-and-leaf plots and robust summary statistics of the percentage of observations that were in error and the percentage of errors that favored the observers' hypotheses (Rosenthal & Rosnow, 1975; Tukey, 1977). Tukey (1977) developed the stem-and-leaf plot as a special form of frequency distribution to facilitate the inspection of a batch of data. Each number in the data batch is made up of one stem and one leaf, but each stem may serve several leaves. Thus, the seventh stem under recording error, a 1., is followed by two leaves of 59 and 69, representing the numbers 1.59 and 1.69. The first digit is the stem, the next digit(s) the leaf. The eye takes in a stem-and-leaf plot as it does any other frequency distribution, but the original data are preserved with greater precision in a stem-and-leaf plot than would be the case with ordinary frequency distributions.

TABLE 3.7
Recording Errors in 27 Studies

Study	Observers (N = 711)	Recordings (N = 219,296)	Errors (N = 23,605)	Error Percentage	Bias Percentage
(1) Kennedy & Uphoff, 1939	28	11,125	126	1.13	68
(2) Rosenthal et al., 1964	30	3,000	20	0.67	75
(3) Weiss, 1967	34	1,770	30	1.69	85
(4) Persinger et al., 1968	11	828	6	0.72	67
(5) Jacob, 1969	36	1,260	40	3.17	60
(6) Todd, 1971	6	864	2	0.23	50
(7) Glass, 1971	4	96	4	4.17	33
(8) Hawthorne, 1972	18	1,009	16	1.59	19
(9) McConnell, 1955	393	18,000	0	0.00	—
(10) Rosenthal & Hall, 1968	5	5,012	41	0.82	—
(11) Doctor, 1968	15	9,600	39	0.41	—
(12) Compton, 1970	9	3,794	36	0.95	—
(13) Howland, 1970	9	360	9	2.50	—
(14) Mayo, 1972	15	688	0	0.00	—
(15) Eisner et al., 1974	12	9,600	66	0.69	—
(16) Rusch et al., 1978	2	46,079	22,339	48.48	—
(17) Marvell, 1979	2	2,156	52	2.41	—
(18) Fleming & Anttonen, 1971	—	89,980	558	0.62	—
(19) Goldberg, 1978	—	5,600	40	0.71	—
(20) Tobias, 1979	—	4,221	141	3.34	—
(21) Tobias, 1979	—	4,254	40	0.94	—
(22) Johnson & Adair, 1970	12	—	—	—	62
(23) Johnson & Adair, 1972	12	—	—	—	58
(24) Ennis, 1974	42	—	—	—	74
(25) Rusch et al., 1974	2	—	—	—	36
(26) Johnson & Ryan, 1976	6	—	—	—	91
(27) Johnson & Ryan, 1976	8	—	—	—	65
Median	12	3,794	39	.94[a]	.64[b]

a. Median weighted by number of recordings = .62.
b. Median weighted by number of recordings = .68.

From Tables 3.7, 3.8, and 3.9 we note that the typical rate of making recording errors is about 1% but, that in an occasional study, the error rate can climb to an extraordinary level of over 48%. Normally we might expect an error rate that high when data are recorded from an analogue rather than a digital mechanism. Thus reading an analogue thermometer as 98.6 could be interpreted as wrong when a digital read-out tells us that the "true" temperature is 98.63. Extraordinary error rates may have more to say about an overly precise criterion than about any practical problem of measurement.

These same three tables also suggest that, of the observational errors that are made, about two-thirds support the observer's hypothesis when only half should do so if the observers were unbiased. (When each study was weighted by the number of errors made, the overall test that bias was nonzero yielded $Z = 4.88$, $p < .000001$.)

TABLE 3.8
Stem-and-Leaf Plots of Recording Error and Bias Rates
(in percentages)

Recording Error									Bias					
Stem	Leaf								Stem	Leaf				
48.	48[a]								9	1				
									8	5				
4.	17[a]								7	4 5				
3.									6	0 2 5 7 8				
3.[b]	17 34								5	0 8				
2.	50								4					
2.[b]	41								3	3 6				
1.	59 69								2					
1.[b]	13								1	9				
0.	62 67 69 71 72 82 94 95													
0.[b]	00 00 23 41													

a. Stems between 4 and 48 are omitted to save space.
b. Stems were divided into upper and lower halves to spread out the distribution.

TABLE 3.9
Summary Statistics for Recording Error and Bias

Statistic	Recording Error (in percentages)	Bias (in percentages)
Maximum	48.48[a]	91
Quartile 3 (Q_3)	2.46	74
Median (Q_2)	0.94	64
Quartile 1 (Q_1)	0.64	46
Minimum	0.00	19
$Q_3 - Q_1$	1.82	28
$\hat{\sigma}[.75(Q_3 - Q_1)]$	1.36	21
S	10.35	20
Mean	3.58	60
N	21	14

a. This value is a marked outlier; i.e., it deviates from the rest of the distribution of recording error rates at p much less than .001. The mean of the distribution dropping the highest and lowest scores is 1.41.

No one should be surprised to learn that data are sometimes wrongly recorded. Now, however, we have some idea of how often these errors occur. The typical rate of 1% errors is low enough that, even if the errors were undetected, the conclusions of our studies would not be greatly affected. In several studies, analyzing the data with and without the errors corrected made no difference although biased errors would occasionally push a result over the magic .05 cliff (Rosenthal & Gaito, 1963, 1964). Investigators emphasizing confidence intervals, effect sizes, and obtained levels of p will be less misled by the presence of some typical degree of error in their data than will investigators following a strict null hypothesis decision procedure (Snedecor & Cochran, 1967, page 28).

Several implications flow from the results of Tables 3.7, 3.8, and 3.9. We should continue to keep track of error rates and the size of observer bias and do what we can to reduce our errors. Getting all the errors out is probably not possible or even desirable from a cost/benefit perspective. It costs something to reduce errors, and it probably costs more and more to get rid of each error as there are fewer of them left. We may not feel it to be wise to give up half our research to be able to pay for bringing our accuracy rate from 99.0% to 99.9%, if that should be the price.

Finally, there is something we can do to keep our errors random with respect to our hypotheses, so that they will not increase Type I errors. We can keep the processes of data collection and analysis as blind as possible for as long as possible.

Of course it is no basis for rejoicing to learn that errors may be nearly universal even if they are not typically very damaging in their magnitude. Yet one desirable consequence of widespread awareness of error might be to generate a more task-oriented attitude toward error than is currently widely shared. Too often the current attitude is that poor scientists (they) make errors; good scientists (we) don't make errors. Given this attitude, when we reanalyze others' data, we may wax indignant or even triumphant when we find errors. Our goal, it should be remembered, is not to show someone's answer wrong; our goal is to get the answer right. Perhaps if we held this more task-oriented attitude, investigators would be more willing to let others examine their data. Then, perhaps, there would be a drop in the frequency of raw-data-consuming fires, a frequency that exceeds the limits of credibility (Wolins, 1962).

II.B. Evaluating the Quality of Research Results

In our earlier discussion of the reliability of retrieval we examined evidence relevant to the accuracy of coding of various features of the studies retrieved. High rates of coder agreement were found for such variables as subjects' average age and the periodical in which the study appeared. Lower agreement was found for features requiring a greater degree of personal judgment. In this section we continue the discussion of reliability but with an emphasis now not on what the study did, but how well the study investigated its topic.

One of the major criticisms of meta-analyses is that poor studies are summarized as well as good studies. Wise meta-analysts make it their business to locate all the studies, poor as well as good. Wise traditional reviewers do the same. Once all the retrievable studies have been found, decisions can be made about the use of any study. Precisely the same decision must be made about every study retrieved: How shall this study be weighted? Dropping a study is simply assigning a weight of zero. If there is a dimension of quality of study (e.g., internal validity, external validity, and so on) then there can be a corresponding system of weighting. If we think a study is twice as good as another, we can weight it twice as heavily or four times more heavily, and so forth.

There is a danger, however, in assigning quality weights to studies, i.e., that we will assign high weights to studies whose results we favor and low weights to those we do not favor (Glass, 1976). The ideal solution is to have each study coded by several excellent methodologists who have no special investment in the area being investigated. Their quality assessments would be made twice; once based only on their reading of the methods section and once based on their reading of the methods plus results section. The reason for the first rating is to ensure that at least one judgment of quality is made before the judge has learned the results of the study. One should be able to assess at least the design features relevant to both internal and external validity before reading the results.

The specific judgments to ask of our methodologists can range from the most general question of overall quality rated on a 9-point rating scale, to intermediate level questions of quality of design, quality of statistical analysis, quality of ecological validity, and the like, all rated on a 9-point scale, to a series of very specific questions such as: Was random assignment of subjects employed? Was the assumption of independence of errors in the analysis of variance met? Whether highly specific variables are judged or not, in the end one overall variable (or a smallish number of fairly general variables) relevant to quality will be constructed and will be correlated with size of the effect obtained (Glass, et al., 1981; Rosenthal & Rubin, 1978).

Glass et al. (1981) have presented convincing evidence that, in the typical meta-analysis, there is no strong relation between the quality of the study and the average size of the effect obtained. Nevertheless, whether such a relation exists should be assessed specifically for each question being addressed meta-analytically. Once our methodologists have assessed each study for quality, we must assess the assessors. The assessment is made empirically by determining their reliability. We do not expect reliability coefficients to be extremely high for complex judgments of research quality (Fiske, 1983). Nevertheless we need to know the reliability for several reasons. Perhaps the main reason is that knowing the reliability suggests whether we will need to increase our sample of judges of research quality.

II.C. The Reliability of Judgments of Quality

II.C.1. Effective reliability. Suppose we had available two judges of the quality of the studies in our meta-analysis. The correlation coefficient reflecting the reliability of the two judges' ratings would be computed to give us our best (and only) estimate of the correlation likely to be obtained between any two judges drawn from the same population of judges. This correlation coefficient, then, is clearly useful; it is not, however, a very good estimate of the reliability of our variable, which is not the rating of quality made by a single judge but rather the mean of two judges' ratings. Suppose, for example, that the correlation between our two judges' ratings of quality were .50; the reliability of the mean of the two judges' ratings, the "effective" reliability, would then be .67 not .50. Intuition suggests that we should gain in reliability in adding the ratings of a second judge because the second judge's random errors should tend to cancel the first judge's random errors. Intuition suggests further that adding more judges, all of whom agree with one another to about the same degree, defined by a mean inter-judge correlation coefficient of .50 for this example, should further increase our "effective" reliability. Our intuition would be supported by an old and well-known result reported independently by Charles Spearman and William Brown in 1910 (Walker & Lev, 1953). With notation altered to suit our current purpose, the well-known Spearman-Brown result is:

$$R = \frac{nr}{1 + (n - 1)r} \qquad [3.1]$$

where   R = "effective" reliability
        n = number of judges
        r = mean reliability among all n judges (i.e., mean of n $(n - 1)/2$ correlations).

Use of this formula assumes that a comparable group of judges would show comparable mean reliability among themselves and with the actual group of judges available to us. This assumption is virtually the same as that all pairs of judges show essentially the same degree of reliability.

As an aid to investigators employing these and related methods, Table 3.10 has been prepared employing the Spearman-Brown formula.

The table gives the effective reliability, R, for each of several values of n, the number of judges making the observations, and r, the mean reliability among the judges. It is intended to facilitate getting approximate answers to each of the following questions:

(1) Given an obtained or estimated mean reliability, r, and a sample of n judges, what is the approximate effective reliability, R, of the mean of the judges' ratings? The value of R is read from the table at the intersection of the appropriate row (n) and column (r).

(2) Given the value of the obtained or desired effective reliability, R, and the number, n, of judges available, what will be the approximate value of the required mean reliability, r? The table is entered in the row corresponding to the n of judges available and is read across until the value of R closest to the one desired is reached. The value of r is then read as the corresponding column heading.

TABLE 3.10
Effective Reliability of the Mean of Judges' Ratings

Number of Judges (n)	Mean Reliability (r)																			
	.03	.05	.10	.15	.20	.25	.30	.35	.40	.45	.50	.55	.60	.65	.70	.75	.80	.85	.90	.95
1	03	05	10	15	20	25	30	35	40	45	50	55	60	65	70	75	80	85	90	95
2	06	10	18	26	33	40	46	52	57	62	67	71	75	79	82	86	89	92	95	97
3	08	14	25	35	43	50	56	62	67	71	75	79	82	85	88	90	92	94	96	98
4	11	17	31	41	50	57	63	68	73	77	80	83	86	88	90	92	94	96	97	*
5	13	21	36	47	56	62	68	73	77	80	83	86	88	90	92	94	95	97	98	*
6	16	24	40	51	60	67	72	76	80	83	86	88	90	92	93	95	96	97	98	*
7	18	27	44	55	64	70	75	79	82	85	88	90	91	93	94	95	97	98	98	*
8	20	30	47	59	67	73	77	81	84	87	89	91	92	94	95	96	97	98	98	*
9	22	32	50	61	69	75	79	83	86	88	90	92	93	94	95	96	97	98	*	*
10	24	34	53	64	71	77	81	84	87	89	91	92	94	95	96	97	98	98	*	*
12	27	39	57	68	75	80	84	87	89	91	92	94	95	96	97	97	98	*	*	**
14	30	42	61	71	78	82	86	88	90	92	93	94	95	96	97	98	98	*	*	**
16	33	46	64	74	80	84	87	90	91	93	94	95	96	97	97	98	98	*	*	**
18	36	49	67	76	82	86	89	91	92	94	95	96	96	97	98	98	*	*	*	**
20	38	51	69	78	83	87	90	92	93	94	95	96	97	97	98	98	*	*	*	**
24	43	56	73	81	86	89	91	93	94	95	96	97	97	98	98	*	*	*	**	**
28	46	60	76	83	88	90	92	94	95	96	97	97	98	98	98	*	*	*	**	**
32	50	63	78	85	89	91	93	95	96	96	97	98	98	98	*	*	*	*	**	**
36	53	65	80	86	90	92	94	95	96	97	97	98	98	*	*	*	*	**	**	**
40	55	68	82	88	91	93	94	96	96	97	98	98	98	*	*	*	*	**	**	**
50	61	72	85	90	93	94	96	96	97	98	98	98	*	*	*	*	**	**	**	**
60	65	76	87	91	94	95	96	97	98	98	98	*	*	*	*	*	**	**	**	**
80	71	81	90	93	95	96	97	98	98	98	*	*	*	*	*	**	**	**	**	**
100	76	84	92	95	96	97	98	98	98	*	*	*	*	*	**	**	**	**	**	**

NOTE: Decimal points have been omitted.
*Approximately .99.
**Approximately 1.00.

(3) Given an obtained or estimated mean reliability, r, and the obtained or desired effective reliability, R, what is the approximate number (n) of judges required? The table is entered in the column corresponding to the mean reliability, r, and is read down until the value of R closest to the one desired is reached. The value of n is then read as the corresponding row title.

Examples of each of the preceding questions may be useful:

(1) Meta-analysts want to work with a quality variable believed to show a mean reliability of .5 and they can afford only 4 judges at the moment. They believe they should go ahead with their study only if the effective reliability will reach or exceed .75. Shall they go ahead? Answer: Yes, because Table 3.10 shows R to be .80 for an n of 4 and an r of .5.

(2) Meta-analysts who will settle for an effective reliability no less than .9 have a sample of 20 judges available. In their selection of quality variables to be judged by these observers, what should be their minimally acceptable mean reliability? Answer: .3.

(3) Meta-analysts who know their choice of variables to have a mean reliability of .4 want to achieve an effective reliability of .85 or higher. How many judges must be allowed for in their preparation of a research budget? Answer: 9.

II.C.1.a. Product moment correlations. It should be noted that the mean reliability (r) of Table 3.10 is to be a product moment correlation coefficient such as Pearson's r or its special cases, the Spearman rank correlation (rho), the point biserial r, or the phi coefficient. It is not appropriate to employ such indices of reliability as percentage or proportion agreement; e.g., number of agreements (A) divided by the sum of agreements (A) and disagreements (D), $A/(A + D)$ or net agreements, $(A - D)/(A + D)$. These indices should not only be avoided in any use of Table 3.10, but they should be avoided in general because of the greatly misleading results that they can yield. For example, suppose two judges are to evaluate 100 field studies for the presence or absence of external validity. If both the judges see external validity in 98 of the field studies and disagree only twice, they would show 98% agreement; yet the χ^2 testing the significance of the product moment correlation phi would be essentially zero! Thus two judges who shared the same bias (e.g., almost all field studies are externally valid) could consistently earn nearly perfect agreement scores while actually correlating essentially zero with one another (phi = .01).

II.C.2. Reliability and analysis of variance. When there are only two judges whose reliability is to be evaluated it is hard to beat the convenience of a product moment correlation coefficient as an appropriate index of reliability. As the number of judges grows larger, however, working with correlation coefficients can become inconvenient. For example, suppose we employed 40 judges and wanted to compute both their mean reliability (r) and

their effective reliability (R). Table 3.10 could get us R from knowing r but
to get r we would have to compute $(40 \times 39)/2 = 780$ correlation coefficients. That is not hard work for computers, but averaging the 780 coefficients to get r is very hard work for investigators or their programmers.
There is an easier way and it involves the analysis of variance.

Table 3.11 shows a simple example of three judges rating the quality of
five studies on a scale of 1 to 7, and Table 3.12 shows the analysis of variance of these data. Our computations require only the use of the last
column, the column of mean squares (Guilford, 1954). Examination of computational formulas 3.2 and 3.3 given below shows that they tell how well
the judges can discriminate among the sampling units (e.g., studies) minus
the judges' disagreements controlling for judges' rating bias or main effects
(e.g., MS encoders − MS residuals), divided by a standardizing quantity.

Our estimate of R, the effective reliability of the ratings of *all* the judges
is given by

$$R\,(\text{est.}) = \frac{\text{MS studies} - \text{MS residual}}{\text{MS studies}} \qquad [3.2]$$

Our estimate of r, the mean reliability or the reliability of a *single* average
judge is given by

$$r\,(\text{est.}) = \frac{\text{MS studies} - \text{MS residual}}{\text{MS studies} + (n - 1)\text{MS residual}} \qquad [3.3]$$

TABLE 3.11
Judges' Ratings of Research Quality

| Studies | Judges | | | |
	A	B	C	Σ
1	5	6	7	18
2	3	6	4	13
3	3	4	6	13
4	2	2	3	7
5	1	4	4	9
Σ	14	22	24	60

TABLE 3.12
Analysis of Variance of Judges' Ratings

Source	SS	df	MS
Studies	24.0	4	6.00
Judges	11.2	2	5.60
Residual	6.8	8	0.85

where n is the number of judges as before (equation 3.3 is known as the intraclass correlation). For our example of Tables 3.11 and 3.12 we have

$$R \text{ (est.)} = \frac{6.00 - 0.85}{6.00} = .858$$

and

$$r \text{ (est.)} = \frac{6.00 - 0.85}{6.00 + (3 - 1)0.85} = .669$$

In the present example it will be easy to compare the results of the analysis of variance approach with the more cumbersome correlational approach. Thus the correlations (r) between pairs of judges (r_{AB}, r_{BC} and r_{AC}) are .645, .582, and .800 respectively, and the mean intercorrelation is .676 which differs by only .007 from the estimate (.669) obtained by means of the analysis of variance approach.

If we were employing only the correlational approach we would apply the Spearman-Brown formula (equation 3.1) to our mean reliability of .676 to find R, the effective reliability. The result is

$$R = \frac{(3)(.676)}{1 + (3 - 1)(.676)} = .862$$

which differs by only .004 from the estimate (.858) obtained by means of the analysis of variance approach. In general, the differences obtained between the correlational approach and the analysis of variance approach are quite small (Guilford, 1954).

It should be noted that in our present simple example, the correlational approach was not an onerous one to employ, with only three correlations to compute. As the number of judges increased, however, we would find ourselves more and more grateful for the analysis of variance approach.

II.C.2.a. Quality of research and effect size. As an additional example of the computation of reliability from analysis of variance, we examine some data summarized by Glass et al. (1981). For 11 different meta-analyses, separate estimates of mean effect size were given for studies judged to be of high, medium, or low internal validity. On the basis of an analysis weighting the 11 studies equally, the mean effect sizes (Δ) were found to be .42, .34, and .57 respectively, for the high, medium, and low quality studies. The analogous medians were .48, .31, and .59. These results suggest no very great linear effect of quality on mean effect size obtained. (Note that though "poor" studies tend to show larger effects, "good" studies tend to show larger effects than intermediate studies.)

The question we want to put to these data is: What is the degree of agreement, in the sense of reliability coefficients, among the three levels of quality? We address the question via analysis of variance and find:

$$R \text{ (est.)} = \frac{MS \text{ studies} - MS \text{ residual}}{MS \text{ studies}} = \frac{.1821 - .0571}{.1821} = .686$$

Therefore, the effective reliability of the differentiation of the 11 meta-analyses is seen to be about .69. Our estimate of the mean reliability (r), or the reliability of a single level of quality is:

$$r \text{ (est.)} = \frac{MS \text{ studies} - MS \text{ residual}}{MS \text{ studies} + (n - 1)MS \text{ residual}} = \frac{.1821 - .0571}{.1821 + (3 - 1).0571} = .422$$

In this example, the correlation of the high quality with the medium quality studies was .558, while the correlations of high with low and medium with low quality studies were .381, and .376 respectively. The mean of these three reliabilities was .438, a value quite close to that obtained from the analysis of variance (.422). All in all, the low quality studies do not agree as well with the others (the high and the medium) in differentiating the meta-analyses.

II.C.3. Reliability and principal components. In situations where the ratings made by all judges have been intercorrelated, and a principal components analysis is readily available, another very efficient alternative to estimate the reliability of the total set of judges is available. Armor (1974) has developed an index, theta (θ), that is based on the unrotated first principal component (where a principal component is a factor extracted from a correlation matrix employing unity [1.00] in the diagonal of the correlation matrix). The formula for theta is

$$\theta \text{eta} (\theta) = \frac{n}{n - 1} \left[\frac{L - 1}{L} \right] \qquad [3.4]$$

where n is the number of judges and L is the latent root or eigenvalue of the first unrotated principal component. The latent root is the sum of the squared factor loadings for any given factor and can be thought of as the amount of variance in the judges' ratings accounted for by that factor. Factor analytic computer programs generally give latent roots or eigenvalues for each factor extracted so that θ is very easy to obtain in practice.

II.C.4. Reporting reliabilities. Assuming we have done our reliability analyses well, how shall we report our results? Ideally, reports of reliability analyses should include both the mean reliability (the reliability of a single judge) and the effective reliability (reliability of the total set of judges or of the mean judgments). The reader needs to know the latter reliability (R) because that is, in fact, the reliability of the variable employed in most cases. However, if this reliability is reported without explanation, the reader may not be aware that the reliability of any one judge's ratings are likely to be lower, often substantially so. A reader may note a reported reliability of .80 based on 12 judges and decide that the variable is sufficiently reliable for his or her purposes. This reader may then employ a single judge only to find later that this single judge was operating at a reliability of .25, not .80. Reporting both reliabilities avoids such misunderstandings.

II.C.4.a. Split-sample reliabilities. A related source of misunderstanding is the reporting of correlations between a mean judge of one type with a mean judge of another type. For example, suppose we had 10 male and 10 female judges, or 10 student and 10 faculty judges. One sometimes sees in the literature the reliability of the mean male and mean female judge or of the mean student and mean faculty judge. Such a correlation of the mean ratings made by all judges of one type with the mean ratings made by judges of another type can be very useful, but they should not be reported as reliabilities without the explanation that these correlations might be substantially higher than the average correlation between any one male and any one female judge or between any one student and any one faculty judge. The reasons for this are those discussed in the earlier section on effective reliability.

II.C.4.b. Trimming judges. It sometimes happens that when we examine the intercorrelations among our judges we find one that is very much out of line with all the others. Perhaps this judge tends to obtain negative correlations with other judges or at least to show clearly lower reliabilities with other judges than is typical for the correlation matrix. If this unreliable judge were dropped from the data, the resulting estimates of reliability would be biased, i.e., made to appear too reliable. If a judge must be dropped, the resulting bias can be reduced by equitable trimming. Thus if the lowest agreeing judge is dropped, the highest agreeing judge is also dropped. If the two lowest agreeing judges are dropped, the two highest agreeing judges are also dropped and so on. Experience suggests that when large samples of judges are employed the effects of trimming judges are small as is the need for trimming. When the sample of judges is small, we may feel a stronger need to drop a judge, but doing so is more likely to leave a residual biased estimate of reliability. A safe procedure is to do all analyses with and without the trimming of judges and to report the differences in results from data with and without the trimming. Although the method of trimming judges seems not yet to have been systematically applied, the theoretical foundations for the method can be seen in the writings of Mosteller and Rourke (1973), Tukey (1977), and Hoaglin, Mosteller, and Tukey (1983).

4

Comparing and Combining Research Results

A framework for meta-analytic procedures is described in which the comparing function and the combining function of meta-analytic procedures are distinguished. Procedures are provided for comparing and for combining the tests of significance and the effect size estimates from two or more studies.

I. A FRAMEWORK FOR META-ANALYTIC PROCEDURES

In this chapter we consider in detail the application of various meta-analytic procedures. Before we wax computational, however, it will be useful to consider a general framework for putting into perspective a variety of meta-analytic procedures. Table 4.1 provides a summary of four types of meta-analytic procedures that are applicable to the special case where just two studies are to be evaluated. It is useful to list the two-study case separately because there are some especially convenient computational procedures for this situation. The two columns of Table 4.1 show that there are two major ways to evaluate the results of research studies — in terms of their statistical significance (e.g., p levels) and in terms of their effect sizes (e.g., the difference between means divided by the common standard deviation σ or S, indices employed by Cohen [1969, 1977] and by Glass [1980], or the Pearson r). The two rows of Table 4.1 show that there are two major analytic processes applied to the set of studies to be evaluated: comparing and combining. The cell labeled A in Table 4.1 represents the procedure that evaluates whether the significance level of one study differs significantly from the significance level of the other study. The cell labeled B represents the procedure that evaluates whether the effect size (e.g., d or r) of one study differs significantly from the effect size of the other study. Cells C and D

TABLE 4.1
Four Types of Meta-Analytic Procedures
Applicable to a Set of Two Studies

| | Results Defined in Terms of: | |
	Significance testing	Effect size estimation
Analytic Process		
Comparing studies	A	B
Combining studies	C	D

TABLE 4.2
Six Types of Meta-Analytic Procedures
Applicable to a Set of Three or More Studies

| | Results Defined in Terms of: | |
	Significance testing	Effect size estimation
Analytic Process		
Comparing studies: Diffuse tests	A	B
Comparing studies: Focused tests	C	D
Combining studies	E	F

represent the procedures that are used to estimate the overall level of significance and the average size of the effect, respectively. Illustrations of these procedures will be given below.

Table 4.2 provides a more general summary of six types of meta-analytic procedures that are applicable to the case where three or more studies are to be evaluated. The columns are as in Table 4.1 but the row labeled "Comparing Studies" in Table 4.1 has now been divided into two rows — one for the case of diffuse tests and one for the case of focused tests.

When studies are compared as to their significance levels (Cell A) or their effect sizes (Cell B) by diffuse tests, we learn whether they differ significantly among themselves with respect to significance levels or effect sizes, respectively, but we do not learn how they differ or whether they differ according to any systematic basis. When studies are compared as to their significance levels (Cell C) or their effect sizes (Cell D) by focused tests, or contrasts, we learn whether the studies differ significantly among themselves in a theoretically predictable or meaningful way. Thus important tests of hypotheses can be made by the use of focused tests. Cells E and F of Table 4.2 are simply analogues of Cells C and D of Table 4.1 representing procedures used to estimate overall level of significance and average size of the effect, respectively.

II. META-ANALYTIC PROCEDURES:
TWO INDEPENDENT STUDIES

Even when we have been quite rigorous and sophisticated in the interpretation of the results of a single study, we are often prone to err in the interpretation of two or more studies. For example, Smith may report a significant effect of some social intervention only to have Jones publish a rebuttal demonstrating that Smith was wrong in her claim. A closer look at both their results may show the following:

Smith's Study: $t(78) = 2.21, p < .05, d = .50, r = .24.$
Jones's Study: $t(18) = 1.06, p > .30, d = .50, r = .24.$

Smith's results were more significant than Jones's, to be sure, but the studies were in perfect agreement as to their estimated sizes of effect defined by either d or r. A further comparison of their respective significance levels reveals that these p's are not significantly different ($p = .42$). Clearly Jones was quite wrong in claiming that he had failed to replicate Smith's results. We shall begin this section by considering some procedures for comparing quantitatively the results of two independent studies, i.e., studies conducted with different research participants. The examples in this chapter are in most cases hypothetical, constructed specifically to illustrate a wide range of situations that occur when working on meta-analytic problems.

II.A. Comparing Studies

II.A.1. Significance testing. Ordinarily when we compare the results of two studies we are more interested in comparing their effect sizes than their p values. However, sometimes we cannot do any better than comparing their p values and here is how we do it (Rosenthal & Rubin, 1979a): For each of the two test statistics we obtain a reasonably exact one-tailed p level. All of the procedures described in this chapter require that p levels be recorded as one-tailed. Thus $t(100) = 1.98$ is recorded as $p = .025$, not $p = .05$. Then as an illustration of being reasonably exact, if we obtain $t(30) = 3.03$ we give p as .0025, not as "< .05." Extended tables of the t distribution are helpful here (e.g., Federighi, 1959; Rosenthal & Rosnow, 1984a). For each p, we find Z, the standard normal deviate corresponding to the p value. Since both p's must be one-tailed, the corresponding Z's will have the same sign if both studies show effects in the same direction but different signs if the results are in the opposite direction. The difference between the two Z's when divided by $\sqrt{2}$, yields a new Z that corresponds to the p value that the difference between the Z's could be so large, or larger, if the two Z's did not really differ. Recapping,

$$\frac{Z_1 - Z_2}{\sqrt{2}} \quad \text{is distributed as Z} \qquad [4.1]$$

Example 1. Studies A and B yield results in opposite directions and neither is "significant." One p is .06, one-tailed, the other is .12, one-tailed but in the opposite tail. The Z's corresponding to these p's are found in a table of the normal curve to be +1.56 and −1.18. (Note the opposite signs to indicate results in opposite directions.) Then, from the preceding equation (4.1) we have

$$\frac{Z_1 - Z_2}{\sqrt{2}} = \frac{(1.56) - (-1.18)}{1.41} = 1.94$$

as the Z of the difference between the two p values or their corresponding Z's. The p value associated with a Z of 1.94 is .026 one-tailed or .052 two-tailed. The two p values may be seen to differ significantly, suggesting that we may want to draw different inferences from the results of the two studies.

Example 2. Studies A and B yield results in the same direction and both are significant. One p is .04, the other is .000025. The Z's corresponding to these p's are 1.75 and 4.06. (Since both Z's are in the same tail they have the same sign.) From equation 4.1 we have

$$\frac{Z_1 - Z_2}{\sqrt{2}} = \frac{(4.06) - (1.75)}{1.41} = 1.64$$

as our obtained Z of the difference. The p associated with that Z is .050 one-tailed or .100 two-tailed, so we may want to conclude that the two p values differ significantly or nearly so. It should be emphasized, however, that finding one Z greater than another does not tell us whether that Z was greater because the size of the effect was greater, the size of the study (e.g., N) was greater, or both.

Example 3. Studies A and B yield results in the same direction, but one is "significant" (p = .05) and the other is not (p = .06). This illustrates the worst case scenario for inferential errors where investigators might conclude that the two results are inconsistent because one is significant and the other is not. Regrettably, this example is not merely theoretical. Just such errors have been made and documented (Rosenthal & Gaito, 1963, 1964).

The Z's corresponding to these p's are 1.64 and 1.55. From equation 4.1 we have

$$\frac{Z_1 - Z_2}{\sqrt{2}} = \frac{(1.64) - (1.55)}{1.41} = .06$$

as our obtained Z of the difference between a p value of .05 and .06. The p value associated with this difference is .476 one-tailed or .952 two-tailed. This example shows clearly just how nonsignificant the difference between significant and nonsignificant results can be.

II.A.2. Effect size estimation. When we ask whether two studies are telling the same story, what we usually mean is whether the results (in terms of the estimated effect size) are reasonably consistent with each other or whether they are significantly heterogeneous. The present chapter will emphasize r as the effect size indicator but analogous procedures are available for comparing such other effect size indicators as Hedge's (1981) g or differences between proportions, d' (Hedges, 1928b; Hsu, 1980; Rosenthal & Rubin, 1982a). These will be described and illustrated shortly.

For each of the two studies to be compared we compute the effect size r and find for each of these r's the associated Fisher z_r defined as ½ $\log_e$ [(1 + r)/(1 − r)]. Tables to convert our obtained r's to Fisher z_r's are available in most introductory textbooks of statistics. Then, when N_1 and N_2 represent the number of sampling units (e.g., subjects) in each of our two studies, the quantity

$$\frac{Z_{r_1} - Z_{r_2}}{\sqrt{\dfrac{1}{N_1 - 3} + \dfrac{1}{N_2 - 3}}} \qquad [4.2]$$

is distributed as Z (Snedecor & Cochran, 1967, 1980).

Example 4. Studies A and B yield results in opposite directions with effect sizes of r = .60 (N = 15) and r = −.20 (N = 100), respectively. The Fisher z_r's corresponding to these r's are .69 and −.20, respectively. (Note the opposite signs of the z_r's to correspond to the opposite signs of the r's.) Then from the preceding equation (4.2) we have

$$\frac{Z_{r_1} - Z_{r_2}}{\sqrt{\dfrac{1}{N_1 - 3} + \dfrac{1}{N_2 - 3}}} = \frac{(.69) - (-.20)}{\sqrt{\dfrac{1}{12} + \dfrac{1}{97}}} = 2.91$$

as the Z of the difference between the two effect sizes. The p value associated with a Z of 2.91 is .002 one-tailed or .004 two-tailed. These two effect sizes, then, differ significantly.

Example 5. Studies A and B yield results in the same direction with effect sizes of $r = .70$ (N = 20) and $r = .25$ (N = 95), respectively. The Fisher z_r's corresponding to these r's are .87 and .26, respectively. From equation 4.2 we have

$$\frac{(.87) - (.26)}{\sqrt{\dfrac{1}{17} + \dfrac{1}{92}}} = 2.31$$

as our obtained Z of the difference. The p associated with that Z is .01 one-tailed or .02 two-tailed. Here is an example of two studies that agree on a significant positive relationship between variables X and Y but disagree significantly in their estimates of the size of the relationship.

Example 6. Studies A and B yield effect size estimates of $r = .00$ (N = 17) and $r = .30$ (N = 45), respectively. The Fisher z_r's corresponding to these r's are .00 and .31, respectively. From equation 4.2 we have

$$\frac{(.00) - (.31)}{\sqrt{\dfrac{1}{14} + \dfrac{1}{42}}} = -1.00$$

as our obtained Z of the difference between our two effect size estimates. The p associated with that Z is .16 one-tailed or .32 two-tailed. Here we have an example of two effect sizes, one zero ($r = .00$), the other ($r = .30$) significantly different from zero ($t(43) = 2.06$, $p < .025$ one-tailed), but which do not differ significantly from one another. This illustrates how careful we must be in concluding that results of two studies are heterogeneous just because one is significant and the other is not or because one has a zero estimated effect size and the other does not (Rosenthal & Rosnow, 1984a).

II.A.2.a. Other effect size estimates. Although r is our preferred effect size estimate in this chapter, analogous procedures are available for such other effect size estimates as $(M_1 - M_2)/S$ (Hedges's g) or the difference between proportions, d'. We begin with the case of Hedges's g.

For each of the two studies to be compared, we compute the effect size

$(M_1 - M_2)/S$ (Hedges's g) and the quantity $1/w$ which is the estimated variance of g. We obtain w as follows (Rosenthal & Rubin, 1982a).

$$w = \frac{2(n_1n_2)(n_1 + n_2 - 2)}{(n_1 + n_2)[t^2 + 2(n_1 + n_2 - 2)]} \qquad [4.3]$$

When we have w we can test the significance of the difference between any two independent g's by means of a Z test since

$$\frac{g_A - g_B}{\sqrt{\dfrac{1}{w_A} + \dfrac{1}{w_B}}} \qquad [4.4]$$

is distributed as Z, as shown in somewhat different form in Rosenthal and Rubin (1982a). Note the similarity in structure between equations 4.4 and 4.2. In both cases the differences in effect size are divided by the square root of the sums of the variances of the individual effect sizes.

Example 7. Studies A and B yield results in the same direction with effect sizes of $g = 1.86$ ($t = 4.16$; $N = 20$) and $g = .51$ ($t = 2.49$; $N = 95$), respectively. Assuming that the two conditions being compared within each study are comprised of sample sizes of 10 and 10 in Study A and 47 and 48 in Study B, we first find w for each study.

$$w_A = \frac{2(n_1n_2)(n_1 + n_2 - 2)}{(n_1 + n_2)[t^2 + 2(n_1 + n_2 - 2)]} = \frac{2(10)(10)(10 + 10 - 2)}{(10 + 10)[(4.16)^2 + 2(10 + 10 - 2)]} = 3.38$$

$$w_B = \frac{2(n_1n_2)(n_1 + n_2 - 2)}{(n_1 + n_2)[t^2 + 2(n_1 + n_2 - 2)]} = \frac{2(47)(48)(47 + 48 - 2)}{(47 + 48)[(2.49)^2 + 2(47 + 48 - 2)]} = 22.98$$

Therefore, from equation 4.4:

$$\frac{g_A - g_B}{\sqrt{\dfrac{1}{w_A} + \dfrac{1}{w_B}}} = \frac{1.86 - .51}{\sqrt{\dfrac{1}{3.38} + \dfrac{1}{22.98}}} = 2.32$$

as our obtained Z of the difference. The p associated with that Z is .01 one-tailed or .02 two-tailed. Here is an example of two studies that agree there is a significant effect of the independent variable, but disagree significantly in their estimates of the size of the effect.

Suppose that in the present example we had found Studies A and B but that no effect sizes had been computed — only t tests. If our preference were to work with r as our effect size estimate we could get r from equation 2.16. Recall that t's and N's for these studies were 4.16 (N = 20) and 2.49 (N = 95), respectively; then we can get the two r's:

$$r_A = \sqrt{\frac{t^2}{t^2 + df}} = \sqrt{\frac{(4.16)^2}{(4.16)^2 + 18}} = .70$$

$$r_B = \sqrt{\frac{t^2}{t^2 + df}} = \sqrt{\frac{(2.49)^2}{(2.49)^2 + 93}} = .25$$

We could compare these r's easily; in fact we did so in example 5. The Z we obtained there was 2.31, very close to the Z we obtained when comparing g's (Z = 2.32).

Now suppose we had remembered how to get r from t but had forgotten how to compare two r's. If we recalled how to compare two g's we could convert our r's to g's by means of equation 2.27:

$$g = \frac{r}{\sqrt{1 - r^2}} \times \sqrt{\frac{df(n_1 + n_2)}{n_1 n_2}} \qquad [2.27]$$

For the present example:

$$g_A = \frac{.70}{\sqrt{1 - (.70)^2}} \times \sqrt{\frac{18(10 + 10)}{(10)(10)}} = 1.86$$

$$g_B = \frac{.25}{\sqrt{1 - (.25)^2}} \times \sqrt{\frac{93(47 + 48)}{(47)(48)}} = .51$$

Of course, we could also have computed g directly from t by means of equations 2.25 (or 2.26, or 2.5). From equation 2.25 we have:

$$g_A = t \sqrt{\frac{1}{n_1} + \frac{1}{n_2}} = 4.16 \sqrt{\frac{1}{10} + \frac{1}{10}} = 1.86$$

$$g_B = t \sqrt{\frac{1}{n_1} + \frac{1}{n_2}} = 2.49 \sqrt{\frac{1}{47} + \frac{1}{48}} = .51$$

Finally, if we should have Cohen's d available $[(M_1 - M_2)/\sigma]$ and wanted to get g we could do so as follows:

$$g = \frac{d}{\sqrt{\frac{n_1 + n_2}{n_1 + n_2 - 2}}} \qquad [4.5]$$

If our effect size estimate were the difference between proportions (d'), our procedure would be analogous to that when our effect size estimate was Hedges's g. Again we need the estimated variance of the effect size estimate, $1/w$. In this application we estimate w by equation 4.6 which works well unless n_1 or n_2 is very small and p_1 or p_2 is very close to zero or one. If n_1 or n_2 is very small, a conservative procedure is to replace $p(1 - p)$ by its maximal possible value of .25 (i.e., when $p = (1 - p) = .50$ we find $p(1 - p)$ to be at a maximum and equal to .25).

$$w = \frac{n_1 n_2}{n_2 p_1 (1 - p_1) + n_1 p_2 (1 - p_2)} \qquad [4.6]$$

In meta-analytic work, however, we are sometimes unable to obtain the values of n_1 and n_2. Accordingly we employ an approximation to w that depends only on the total study size N and the effect size estimate d' (Rosenthal & Rubin, 1982a):

$$w = \frac{N}{1 - d'^2} \qquad [4.7]$$

This approximation to equation 4.6 holds exactly when p_1 and p_2 are the same amount above and below .5 and when $n_1 = n_2$.

When we have w we can test the significance of the difference between any two independent d''s by means of a Z test since

$$\frac{d'_A - d'_B}{\sqrt{\dfrac{1}{w_A} + \dfrac{1}{w_B}}} \quad \text{is distributed as Z} \qquad [4.8]$$

as shown in somewhat different form in Rosenthal and Rubin (1982a). Just as was the case when effect size estimates were r and g (equations 4.2 and 4.4), the differences in effect size are divided by the square root of the sums of the variances of the individual effect sizes.

Example 8. Studies A and B yield results in the same direction with effect sizes of $d' = .70$ (N = 20) and $d' = .25$ (N = 95), respectively. Assuming that the two conditions being compared within each study are comprised of sample sizes of 10 and 10 in Study A and 47 and 48 in Study B, we find w first from equation 4.6. Then, as a further illustration, we also employ the approximation equation 4.7:

$$w_{A_1} = \frac{n_1 n_2}{n_2 p_1 (1 - p_1) + n_1 p_2 (1 - p_2)} = \frac{(10)(10)}{(10).85(.15) + (10).15(.85)} = 39.22$$

$$w_{B_1} = \frac{n_1 n_2}{n_2 p_1 (1 - p_1) + n_1 p_2 (1 - p_2)} = \frac{(47)(48)}{(48).375(.625) + (47).625(.375)} = 101.32$$

$$w_{A_2} = \frac{N}{1 - d'^2} = \frac{20}{1 - (.70)^2} = \; 39.22, \text{ agreeing perfectly with the result above } (w_{A_1}).$$

$$w_{B_2} = \frac{N}{1 - d'^2} = \frac{95}{1 - (.25)^2} = \; 101.33, \text{ disagreeing only in the second decimal place with the result above } (w_{B_1}) \text{ because this approximation } (w_{B_2}) \text{ assumed } n_1 = n_2 = 47.5 \text{ rather than } n_1 = 47 \text{ and } n_2 = 48 \text{ as in the result above } (w_{B_1}).$$

Now, we can test the difference between our two effect sizes from equation 4.8:

$$\frac{d'_A - d'_B}{\sqrt{\dfrac{1}{w_{A_1}} + \dfrac{1}{w_{B_1}}}} = \frac{.70 - .25}{\sqrt{\dfrac{1}{39.22} + \dfrac{1}{101.32}}} = 2.39$$

as our obtained Z of the difference. The p associated with that Z is .0084 one-tailed or .017 two-tailed. This example, example 8, was selected to reflect the same underlying effect size as example 7 and example 5. The three Z's found by our three methods agreed very well with one another with Z's of 2.39, 2.32, and 2.31, respectively.

II.B. Combining Studies

II.B.1. Significance testing. After comparing the results of any two independent studies, it is an easy matter to combine the p levels of the two studies. Thus we get an overall estimate of the probability that the two p levels might have been obtained if the null hypothesis of no relation between X and Y were true. Many methods for combining the results of two or more studies are available; they will be described later and have been summarized elsewhere (Rosenthal, 1978, 1980). Here it is necessary to give only the simplest and most versatile of the procedures, the method of adding Z's called the Stouffer method by Mosteller and Bush (1954). This method, like the method of comparing p values, asks us first to obtain accurate p levels for each of our two studies and then to find the Z corresponding to each of these p levels. Both p's must be given in one-tailed form and the corresponding Z's will have the same sign if both studies show effects in the same direction. They will have different signs if the results are in the opposite direction. The sum of the two Z's when divided by $\sqrt{2}$, yields a new Z. This new Z corresponds to the p value that the results of the two studies combined (or results even further out in the same tail) could have occurred if the null hypothesis of no relationship between X and Y were true. Recapping,

$$\frac{Z_1 + Z_2}{\sqrt{2}} \quad \text{is distributed as Z} \qquad [4.9]$$

We could weight each Z by its df, its estimated quality, or any other desired weights (Mosteller & Bush, 1954; Rosenthal, 1978, 1980).

The general procedure for weighting Z's is to multiply each Z by any desired weight (assigned before inspection of the data), add the weighted Z's and divide the sum of the weighted Z's by the square root of the sum of the squared weights as follows:

$$\text{Weighted } Z = \frac{w_1 Z_1 + w_2 Z_2}{\sqrt{w_1^2 + w_2^2}} \qquad [4.10]$$

Example 11 will illustrate the application of this procedure.

Example 9. Studies A and B yield results in opposite directions and both are significant. One p is .05, one-tailed, the other is .0000001, one-tailed but in the opposite tail. The Z's corresponding to these p's are found in a table of normal deviates to be -1.64 and 5.20, respectively. (Note the opposite signs to indicate results in opposite directions.) Then from equation 4.9 we have

$$\frac{Z_1 + Z_2}{\sqrt{2}} = \frac{(-1.64) + (5.20)}{1.41} = 2.52$$

as the Z of the combined results of Studies A and B. The p value associated with a Z of 2.52 is .006 one-tailed or .012 two-tailed. Thus the combined p supports the result of the more significant of the two results. If these were actual results we would want to be very cautious in interpreting our combined p both because the two p's were significant in opposite directions and because the two p's were so significantly different from each other. We would try to discover what differences between Studies A and B might have led to results so different.

Example 10. Studies A and B yield results in the same direction but neither is significant. One p is .11, the other is .09 and their associated Z's are 1.23 and 1.34, respectively. From equation 4.9 we have

$$\frac{(1.23) + (1.34)}{1.41} = 1.82$$

as our combined Z. The p associated with that Z is .034 one-tailed or .068 two-tailed.

Example 11. Studies A and B are those of example 9 but now we have found from a panel of experts that Study A earns a weight (w_1) of 3.4 on assessed internal validity while Study B earns only a weight (w_2) of 0.9. The Z's for Studies A and B had been -1.64 and 5.20 respectively. Therefore, employing equation 4.10 we find

$$\frac{(3.4)(-1.64) + (0.9)(5.20)}{\sqrt{(3.4)^2 + (0.9)^2}} = \frac{-0.896}{3.517} = -0.25$$

as the Z of the combined results of Studies A and B. The p value associated with this Z is .40 one-tailed or .80 two-tailed. Note that weighting has led to a nonsignificant result in this example. In example 9 where there was no weighting (or, more accurately, equal weighting with $w_1 = w_2 = 1$), the p value was significant at $p = .012$ two-tailed.

If the weighting had been by df rather than research quality, and if df for Studies A and B had been 36 and 144 respectively, the weighted Z would have been

$$\frac{(36)(-1.64) + (144)(5.20)}{\sqrt{(36)^2 + (144)^2}} = \frac{689.76}{148.43} = 4.65$$

This result shows the combined Z ($p < .000002$ one-tailed) to have been moved strongly in the direction of the Z with the larger df because of the substantial difference in df between the two studies. Note that when weighting Z's by df we have decided to have the size of the study play a very large role in determining the combined p. The role is very large because the size of the study has already entered into the determination of each Z and is therefore entering a second time into the weighting process.

II.B.2. Effect size estimation. When we want to combine the results of two studies, we are at least as interested in the combined estimate of the effect size as we are in the combined probability. Just as was the case when we compared two effect size estimates, we shall consider r as our primary effect size estimate in the combining of effect sizes. However, many other estimates are possible (e.g., Cohen's d, Hedges's g, or Glass's Δ, or differences between proportions, d').

For each of the two studies to be combined, we compute r and the associated Fisher z_r and have

$$\frac{Z_{r_1} + Z_{r_2}}{2} = \bar{Z}_r$$

[4.11]

as the Fisher z_r corresponding to our mean r. We use an r to z_r or z_r to r table to look up the r associated with our mean $\bar{z}_r$. Tables are handier than computing r from z_r from the following: $r = (e^{2z_r} - 1)/(e^{2z_r} + 1)$. Should we want to do so we could weight each z_r by its df, i.e., $N - 3$ (Snedecor & Cochran, 1967; 1980), by its estimated research quality, or by any other weights assigned before inspection of the data.

The weighted mean z_r is obtained as follows:

$$\text{weighted mean } z_r = \frac{w_1 z_{r_1} + w_2 z_{r_2}}{w_1 + w_2} \qquad [4.12]$$

Example 14 will illustrate the application of this procedure.

Example 12. Studies A and B yield results in opposite directions, one r = .80, the other r = $-.30$. The Fisher z_r's corresponding to these r's are 1.10 and -0.31, respectively. From equation (4.10) we have

$$\frac{z_{r_1} + z_{r_2}}{2} = \frac{(1.10) + (-0.31)}{2} = .395$$

as the mean Fisher z_r. From our z_r to r table we find a z_r of .395 associated with an r of .38.

Example 13. Studies A and B yield results in the same direction, one r = .95, the other r = .25. The Fisher z_r's corresponding to these r's are 1.83 and .26, respectively. From equation (4.11) we have

$$\frac{1.83 + .26}{2} = 1.045$$

as the mean Fisher z_r. From our z_r to r table we find a z_r of 1.045 to be associated with an r of .78. Note that if we had averaged the two r's without first transforming them to Fisher z_r's we would have found the mean r to be $(.95 + .25)/2 = .60$, substantially smaller than .78. This illustrates that the use of Fisher's z_r gives heavier weight to r's that are further from zero in either direction.

Example 14. Studies A and B are those of example 6 but now we have decided to weight the studies by their df (i.e., $N - 3$ in this application). Therefore, equation 4.12 can be rewritten to indicate that we are using df as weights as follows:

$$\text{weighted } \bar{z}_r = \frac{df_1 z_{r_1} + df_2 z_{r_2}}{df_1 + df_2} \qquad [4.13]$$

In example 6 we had r's of .00 and .30 based on N's of 17 and 45, respectively. The Fisher z_r's corresponding to our two r's are .00 and .31. Therefore, we find our weighted z_r to be

$$\frac{(17 - 3).00 + (45 - 3).31}{(17 - 3) + (45 - 3)} = \frac{13.02}{56} = .232$$

which corresponds to an r of .23.

Finally, it should be noted that before combining tests of significance and/or effect size estimates, it is very useful first to test the significance of the difference between the two p values or, what is preferable if they are available, the two effect sizes. If the results of the studies do differ we should be most cautious about combining their p values or effect sizes — especially when their results are in opposite directions.

II.B.2.a. Other effect size estimates. All that has been said about the combining of r's applies in principle also to the combining of other effect size estimates. Thus we can average Hedges's g, or Cohen's d, or Glass's Δ, or the difference between proportions, d', or any other effect size estimate, with or without weighting. The difference in practice is that when we combine r's we typically transform them to Fisher's z_r's before combining, while with most other effect size estimates we do not transform them before combining them.

III. META-ANALYTIC PROCEDURES:
ANY NUMBER OF INDEPENDENT STUDIES

Although we can do quite a lot in the way of comparing and combining the results of sets of studies with the procedures given so far, it often happens that we have three or more studies of the same relationship that we want to compare and/or combine. The purpose of this section is to present generalizations of the procedures given in the last section so that we can compare and combine the results of any number of independent studies. Again, the examples are hypothetical, constructed to illustrate a wide range of situations occurring in meta-analytic work in any domain. Often, of course, the number of studies entering into our analyses will be larger than the number required to illustrate the various meta-analytic procedures.

III.A. Comparing Studies: Diffuse Tests

III.A.1. Significance testing. Given three or more p levels to compare we first find the standard normal deviate, Z, corresponding to each p level. All p levels must be one-tailed and the corresponding Z's will have the same sign if all studies show effects in the same direction, but different signs if the results are not all in the same direction. The statistical significance of the heterogeneity of the Z's can be obtained from a χ^2 computed as follows (Rosenthal & Rubin, 1979a):

$$\sum(Z_j - \overline{Z})^2 \text{ is distributed as } \chi^2 \text{ with } K - 1 \text{ df} \qquad [4.14]$$

In this equation Z_j is the Z for any one study, $\overline{Z}$ is the mean of all the Z's obtained, and K is the number of studies being combined.

Example 15. Studies A, B, C, and D yield one-tailed p values of .15, .05, .01, and .001, respectively. Study C, however, shows results opposite in direction from those of studies A, B, and D. From a normal table we find the Z's corresponding to the four p levels to be 1.04, 1.64, −2.33, and 3.09. (Note the negative sign for the Z associated with the result in the opposite direction.) Then, from the preceding equation 4.14 we have

$$\sum(Z_j - \overline{Z})^2 = [(1.04) - (0.86)]^2 + [(1.64) - (0.86)]^2 + [(-2.33) - (0.86)]^2 \\ + [(3.09) - (0.86)]^2 = 15.79$$

as our χ^2 value which for $K - 1 = 4 - 1 = 3$ df is significant at p = .0013. The four p values we compared, then, are clearly significantly heterogeneous.

III.A.2. Effect size estimation. Here we want to assess the statistical heterogeneity of three or more effect size estimates. We again emphasize r as the effect size estimator, but analogous procedures are available for comparing such other effect size estimators as Hedges's (1981) g or differences between proportions (Hedges, 1982b; Hsu, 1980; Rosenthal & Rubin, 1982a). These will be described and illustrated shortly.

For each of the three or more studies to be compared we compute the effect size r, its associated Fisher z_r, and $N - 3$, where N is the number of sampling units on which each r is based. Then the statistical significance of the heterogeneity of the r's can be obtained from a χ^2 (Snedecor & Cochran, 1967, 1980) because

$$\sum(N_j - 3)(z_{r_j} - \overline{z}_r)^2 \text{ is distributed as } \chi^2 \text{ with } K - 1 \text{ df} \qquad [4.15]$$

In this equation z_{r_j} is the Fisher z_r corresponding to any r, and $\overline{z}_r$ is the weighted mean z_r, i.e.,

$$\overline{z}_r = \frac{\sum(N_j - 3)z_{r_j}}{\sum(N_j - 3)} \qquad [4.16]$$

Example 16. Studies A, B, C, and D yield effect sizes of r = .70 (N = 30), r = .45 (N = 45), r = .10 (N = 20) and r = −.15 (N = 25), respectively. The Fisher z_r's corresponding to these r's are found from tables of Fisher z_r to be

.87, .48, .10, and −.15, respectively. The weighted mean z_r is found from the equation just above (4.16) to be

$$\frac{[27(.87) + 42(.48) + 17(.10) + 22(-.15)]}{[27 + 42 + 17 + 22]} = \frac{42.05}{108} = .39$$

Then from the equation for χ^2 above (equation 4.15) we have

$$\sum(N_j - 3)(z_{r_j} - \overline{z}_r)^2 = 27(.87 - .39)^2 + 42(.48 - .39)^2 + 17(.10 - .39)^2$$
$$+ 22(-.15 - .39)^2 = 14.41$$

as our χ^2 value which for $K - 1 = 3$ df is significant at $p = .0024$. The four effect sizes we compared, then, are clearly significantly heterogeneous.

III.A.2.a. Other effect size estimates. Although r is our preferred effect size estimate in this chapter, analogous procedures are available for such other effect size estimates as $(M_1 - M_2)/S$ (Hedges's g) or the difference between proportions (d′). We begin with the case of Hedges's g.

For each of the studies in the set we compute Hedges's g $[(M_1 - M_2)/S]$ and the reciprocal (w) of the estimated variance of g (1/w). We saw in equation 4.3 how to compute w (Rosenthal & Rubin, 1982a):

$$w = \frac{2(n_1n_2)(n_1 + n_2 - 2)}{(n_1 + n_2)[t^2 + 2(n_1 + n_2 - 2)]}$$ [4.3]

Once we have w we can test the heterogeneity of the set of g's because Hedges (1982b) and Rosenthal and Rubin (1982a) have shown that

$$\sum w_j(g_j - \overline{g})^2 \text{ is distributed approximately as } \chi^2 \text{ with } K - 1 \text{ df} \quad [4.17]$$

The quantity $\overline{g}$ is the weighted mean g defined as

$$\overline{g} = \frac{\sum w_j g_j}{\sum w_j}$$ [4.18]

Note the similarity in structure between equations 4.17 and 4.15 and between 4.18 and 4.16. Equation 4.17 will be an adequate approximation in most circumstances but it will lose some accuracy when sample sizes are very small and t statistics are large.

Example 17. Studies A, B, C, and D yield effect sizes of $g = 1.89$ (N = 30), $g = .99$ (N = 45), $g = .19$ (N = 20) and $g = -.29$ (N = 25), respectively. To employ equations 4.17 and 4.18 we will need to compute w for each effect size. Equation 4.3 showing how to compute w requires knowing the sample sizes of the two groups being compared in each study (n_1 and n_2) as well as the results of the t test. If the t tests were not available we could compute our own from equations 2.4, 2.5, 2.25, or 2.26, for example:

$$t = \frac{g}{\sqrt{\dfrac{1}{n_1} + \dfrac{1}{n_2}}} \qquad [4.19]$$

If the n_1 and n_2 values are not reported but N (i.e., $n_1 + n_2$) is known and if it is reasonable to assume approximately equal sample sizes, we can replace n_1 and n_2 by N/2. In that case equation 4.19 simplifies to

$$t = g \times \frac{\sqrt{N}}{2} \qquad [4.20]$$

and equation 4.3 simplifies to

$$w = \frac{N(N-2)}{2(t^2 + 2N - 4)} \qquad [4.21]$$

Since in the present example we were not given n_1, n_2, or t for studies A, B, C, and D, we employ equation 4.20 to obtain t and equation 4.21 to obtain w for each study. Table 4.3 shows the results of these computations which are shown in detail only for Study A for which N = 30 and g = 1.89. From equation 4.20 we find

$$t = g \times \frac{\sqrt{N}}{2} = 1.89 \times \frac{\sqrt{30}}{2} = 5.18$$

TABLE 4.3
Work Table for Comparing Four Effect Sizes (g)

Study	N	g^a	t^b	t^2	w^c	wg
A	30	1.89	5.18	26.79	5.07	9.58
B	45	.99	3.32	11.03	9.97	9.87
C	20	.19	.42	.18	4.98	.95
D	25	−.29	−.72	.53	6.18	−1.79
Σ	120	2.78	8.20	38.53	26.20	18.61

a. Obtainable from: $g = \dfrac{2t}{\sqrt{N}}$ (from equation 4.20).

b. Obtainable from: $t = \dfrac{g\sqrt{N}}{2}$ (equation 4.20).

c. Obtainable from: $w = \dfrac{N(N-2)}{2(t^2 + 2N - 4)}$ (equation 4.21).

From equation 4.21 we find:

$$w = \frac{N(N - 2)}{2(t^2 + 2N - 4)} = \frac{30(28)}{2(5.18^2 + 2(30) - 4)} = 5.07$$

Before we can employ equation 4.17, our χ^2 test for heterogeneity, we must find $\bar{g}$, the weighted mean g (see equation 4.18), which can be found from the appropriate entries in the row of sums of Table 4.3:

$$\bar{g} = \frac{\sum w_j g_j}{\sum w_j} = \frac{18.61}{26.20} = .71$$

Now we can employ equation 4.17 to compute χ^2:

$$\sum w_j(g_j - \bar{g})^2 = 5.07(1.89 - .71)^2 + 9.97(.99 - .71)^2 + 4.98(.19 - .71)^2 +$$
$$6.18(-.29 - .71)^2 = 15.37$$

a χ^2 value which, for $K - 1 = 3$ df, is significant at $p = .0015$. The four effect sizes we compared, then, are clearly significantly heterogeneous.

The four effect sizes of this example were chosen to be the equivalents in units of g to the effect sizes of example 16 which were in units of r. The $\chi^2(3)$ based on g was somewhat larger (by 7%) than the $\chi^2(3)$ based on r and the p of .0015 is slightly more significant than that for example 16 (.0024). The agreement is close enough for practical purposes but we should not expect perfect agreement. Incidentally, if we have available a set of r's and want to convert them to g's, still assuming approximately equal sample sizes within each condition, we can simplify the conversion equation 2.27 to the following:

$$g = \frac{2r}{\sqrt{1 - r^2}} \times \sqrt{\frac{N - 2}{N}} \qquad [4.22]$$

Should we want to convert g's to r's we can analogously simplify the conversion equation 2.28 to the following:

$$r = \sqrt{\frac{g^2 N}{g^2 N + 4(N - 2)}} \qquad [4.23]$$

If our effect size estimate were the difference between proportions (d'), our procedure would be analogous to that when our effect size estimate was Hedges's g. For each of the studies in the set we compute d' and the reciprocal (w) of the estimated variance of d' (1/w). The basic estimate of w is provided by equation 4.6 which works well unless n_1 or n_2 is very small and

p_1 or p_2 is very close to zero or one. If n_1 or n_2 is very small, a conservative procedure is to replace $p(1 - p)$ by its maximal possible value of .25. We give equation 4.6 again:

$$w = \frac{n_1n_2}{n_2p_1(1 - p_1) + n_1p_2(1 - p_2)} \qquad [4.6]$$

The approximation to this expression that depends only on the total study size (N) and the effect size estimate d' was given earlier as equation 4.7:

$$w = \frac{N}{1 - d'^2} \qquad [4.7]$$

This approximation to equation 4.6 holds exactly when p_1 and p_2 are the same amount above and below .5 and when $n_1 = n_2$.

Once we have w we can test the heterogeneity of the set of d''s by means of equation 4.17 (Rosenthal & Rubin, 1982a) but substituting d' for g:

$$\sum w_j(d' - \bar{d}')^2 \quad \text{is distributed approximately as } \chi^2 \text{ with } K - 1 \text{ df.} \qquad [4.24]$$

The quantity $\bar{d}'$ is the weighted mean d' defined as:

$$\bar{d}' = \frac{\sum w_jd'_j}{\sum w_j} \qquad [4.25]$$

a quantity defined analogously to $\bar{g}$ (see equation 4.18).

Example 18. Studies A, B, C, and D yield effect sizes of $d' = .70, .45, .10,$ and $-.15$, respectively. Table 4.4 shows the results of the computations of w for each of the studies. To illustrate these computations for Study A we employ equation 4.7 as follows:

$$w = \frac{N}{1 - d'^2} = \frac{30}{1 - (.70)^2} = 58.82$$

Before we can employ equation 4.24, our χ^2 test for heterogeneity, we must find $\bar{d}'$, the weighted mean d' (equation 4.25), which can be found from the appropriate entries in the row of sums of Table 4.4:

$$\bar{d}' = \frac{\sum w_jd'_j}{\sum w_j} = \frac{64.751}{161.03} = .40$$

TABLE 4.4
Work Table for Comparing Four Effect Sizes (d′)

Study	N	d′	d′°	1 − d′°	w^a	wd′
A	30	.70	.4900	.5100	58.82	41.174
B	45	.45	.2025	.7975	56.43	25.394
C	20	.10	.0100	.9900	20.20	2.020
D	25	−.15	.0225	.9775	25.58	−3.837
Σ	120	1.10	.7250	3.2750	161.03	64.751

a. Obtainable from: $w = \dfrac{N}{1-d'^2}$ (equation 4.7).

TABLE 4.5
Tests for the Heterogeneity of Effect Sizes
Defined as r, g, and d′

	Effect Sizes		
	r	g	d′
Study A	.70	1.89	.70
Study B	.45	.99	.45
Study C	.10	.19	.10
Study D	−.15	−.29	−.15
Median	.28	.59	.28
Unweighted mean	.31[a]	.70	.28
Weighted mean	.37[a]	.71	.40
$\chi^2(3)$	14.41[a]	15.37	14.99
p	.0024	.0015	.0018

a. Based on Fisher's z_r transformation.

Then, employing equation 4.24 we find:

$$\sum w_j(d' - \bar{d}')^2 = 58.82(.70 - .40)^2 + 56.43(.45 - .40)^2$$
$$+ 20.20(.10 - .40)^2 + 25.58(-.15 - .40)^2 = 14.99$$

a χ^2 value which, for $K - 1 = 3$ df is significant at $p = .0018$. The four effect sizes are significantly heterogeneous.

The four effect sizes of this example were chosen to be the equivalents in units of d′ to the effect sizes of example 16 (r) and example 17 (g). Table 4.5 summarizes the data for the three effect size estimates of examples 16, 17, and 18. While the three $\chi^2(3)$ values are not identical, they are quite similar to one another as are the three significance levels. Table 4.5 also suggests that the metric r is quite similar to the metric d′. Indeed, we shall see in the final chapter of this book that when the proportions being compared are the same amount above and below .5 and when $n_1 = n_2$, r computed from such a 2×2 table does indeed equal d′.

III.B. Comparing Studies: Focused Tests

III.B.1. Significance testing. Although we know how to answer the diffuse question of the significance of the differences among a collection of significance levels, we are often able to ask a more focused and more useful question. For example, given a set of p levels for studies of teacher expectancy effects, we might want to know whether results from younger children show greater degrees of statistical significance than do results from older children (Rosenthal & Rubin, 1978). Normally our greater interest would be in the relation between our weights derived from theory and our obtained effect sizes. Sometimes, however, the effect size estimates, along with their sample sizes, are not available. More rarely, we may be intrinsically interested in the relation between our weights and the obtained levels of significance.

As was the case for diffuse tests, we begin by finding the standard normal deviate, Z, corresponding to each p level. All p levels must be one-tailed, and the corresponding Z's will have the same sign if all studies show effects in the same direction. The statistical significance of the contrast testing any specific hypothesis about the set of p levels can be obtained from a Z computed as follows (Rosenthal & Rubin, 1979a):

$$\frac{\sum \lambda_j Z_j}{\sqrt{\sum \lambda_j^2}} \quad \text{is distributed as Z} \qquad [4.26]$$

In this equation λ_j is the theoretically derived prediction or contrast weight for any one study, chosen such that the sum of the λ_j's will be zero, and Z_j is the Z for any one study.

Example 19. Studies A, B, C, and D yield one-tailed p values of $1/10^7$, .0001, .21, and .007, respectively, all with results in the same direction. From a normal table we find the Z's corresponding to the four p levels to be 5.20, 3.72, .81, and 2.45. Suppose that Studies A, B, C, and D had involved differing amounts of peer tutor contact such that Studies A, B, C, and D had involved 8, 6, 4, and 2 hours of contact per month, respectively. We might, therefore, ask whether there was a linear relationship between number of hours of contact and statistical significance of the result favoring peer tutoring. The weights of a linear contrast involving four studies are 3, 1, -1, and -3. (These are obtained from a table of orthogonal polynomials; see, for example, Rosenthal & Rosnow, 1984a.) Therefore, from the preceding equation we have

$$\frac{\sum \lambda_j Z_j}{\sqrt{\sum \lambda_j^2}} = \frac{(3)5.20 + (1)3.72 + (-1).81 + (-3)2.45}{\sqrt{(3)^2 + (1)^2 + (-1)^2 + (-3)^2}} = \frac{11.16}{\sqrt{20}} = 2.50$$

as our Z value, which is significant at p = .006, one-tailed. The four p values, then, tend to grow linearly more significant as the number of hours of contact time increases.

III.B.2. Effect size estimation. Here we want to ask a more focused question of a set of effect sizes. For example, given a set of effect sizes for studies of peer tutoring, we might want to know whether these effects are increasing or decreasing linearly with the number of hours of contact per month. We again emphasize r as the effect size estimator but analogous procedures are available for comparing such other effect size estimators as Hedges's (1981) g or differences between proportions (d') (Rosenthal & Rubin, 1982a). These will be described and illustrated shortly.

As was the case for diffuse tests, we begin by computing the effect size r, its associated Fisher z_r, and N − 3, where N is the number of sampling units on which each r is based. The statistical significance of the contrast, testing any specific hypothesis about the set of effect sizes, can be obtained from a Z computed as follows (Rosenthal & Rubin, 1982a):

$$\frac{\sum \lambda_j z_{r_j}}{\sqrt{\sum \frac{\lambda_j^2}{w_j}}} \quad \text{is distributed as } Z \tag{4.27}$$

In this equation, λ_j is the contrast weight determined from some theory for any one study, chosen such that the sum of the λ_j's will be zero. The z_{r_j} is the Fisher z_r for any one study and w_j is the inverse of the variance of the effect size for each study. For Fisher z_r transformations of the effect size r, the variance is $1/(N_j - 3)$ so $w_j = N_j - 3$.

Example 20. Studies A, B, C, and D yield effect sizes of r = .89, .76, .23, and .59, respectively, all with N = 12. The Fisher z_r's corresponding to these r's are found from tables of Fisher z_r to be 1.42, 1.00, .23, and .68, respectively. Suppose that Studies A, B, C, and D had involved differing amounts of peer tutor contact such that Studies A, B, C, and D had involved 8, 6, 4, and 2 hours of contact per month, respectively. We might, therefore, ask whether there was a linear relationship between number of hours of contact and size of effect favoring peer tutoring. As in example 19, the appropriate weights, or λ's, are 3, 1, −1, and −3. Therefore, from the preceding equation we have

$$\frac{\sum \lambda_j z_{r_j}}{\sqrt{\sum \frac{\lambda_j^2}{w_j}}} = \frac{(3)1.42 + (1)1.00 + (-1).23 + (-3).68}{\sqrt{\frac{(3)^2}{9} + \frac{(1)^2}{9} + \frac{(-1)^2}{9} + \frac{(-3)^2}{9}}} = \frac{2.99}{\sqrt{2.222}} = 2.01$$

as our Z value which is significant at p = .022 one-tailed. The four effect sizes, therefore, tend to grow linearly larger as the number of hours of contact time increases. Interpretation of this relation must be very cautious. After all, studies were not assigned at random to the four conditions of contact hours. Generally, variables moderating the magnitude of effects found should not be interpreted as giving strong evidence for any causal relationships. Moderator relationships can, however, be very valuable in suggesting the possibility of causal relationships, possibilities that can then be studied experimentally or as nearly experimentally as possible.

III.B.2.a. Other effect size estimates. Although r is our preferred effect size estimate in this chapter, analogous procedures are available for such other effect size estimates as $(M_1 - M_2)/S$ (Hedges's g) or the difference between proportions (d'). We begin with the case of Hedges's g.

Once again we compute the reciprocal (w) of the estimated variance of g (1/w) for each study. We employ equation 4.3 when the individual sample sizes (n_1 and n_2) are known and unequal and equation 4.21 when they are unknown or when they are equal. These equations are as follows:

$$w = \frac{2(n_1 n_2)(n_1 + n_2 - 2)}{(n_1 + n_2)[t^2 + 2(n_1 + n_2 - 2)]} \qquad [4.3]$$

$$w = \frac{N(N - 2)}{2(t^2 + 2N - 4)} \qquad [4.21]$$

We employ the computed w's to test the significance of any contrast we may wish to investigate. The quantity:

$$\frac{\sum \lambda_j g_j}{\sqrt{\sum \dfrac{\lambda_j^2}{w_j}}} \qquad \text{is distributed approximately as Z}$$

$$[4.28]$$

an equation that is identical in structure to equation 4.27 (Rosenthal & Rubin, 1982a). In this application w_j is defined as in equations 4.3 or 4.21 and λ_j is the contrast weight we assign to the jth study on the basis of our theory. The only restriction is that the sum of the λ_j's must be zero (Rosenthal & Rosnow, 1984a; in press).

Example 21. Studies A, B, C, and D yield effect sizes of g = 3.56, 2.13, .43, and 1.33, respectively, all with N = 12. As in example 20, we assume 8, 6, 4, and 2 hours of peer tutoring per month were employed in Studies A, B, C, and D, respectively. We ask whether there was a linear relationship between number of hours of contact and size of effect favoring peer tutoring. As in example 20, the appropriate weights, or λ's, are 3, 1, -1, and -3.

TABLE 4.6
Work Table for Computing Contrasts Among Effect Sizes (g)

Study	N	g^a	t^b	t^2	λ^c	λ^2	λg	w^d	$\dfrac{\lambda^2}{w}$
A	12	3.56	6.17	38.02	3	9	10.68	1.03	8.74
B	12	2.13	3.69	13.61	1	1	2.13	1.79	.56
C	12	.43	.74	.55	−1	1	−.43	2.92	.34
D	12	1.33	2.30	5.31	−3	9	−3.99	2.37	3.80
Σ	48	7.45	12.90	57.49	0	20	8.39	8.11	13.44

a. Obtainable from: $g = \dfrac{2t}{\sqrt{N}}$ (from equation 4.20).

b. Obtainable from: $t = \dfrac{g\sqrt{N}}{2}$ (equation 4.20).

c. Determined by theory but with $\Sigma\lambda = 0$.

d. Obtainable from: $w = \dfrac{N(N-2)}{2(t^2 + 2N - 4)}$ (equation 4.21).

Table 4.6 lists the ingredients required to compute our test of significance (Z) for the contrast and reminds us of the formulas that can be used to obtain the various quantities. Now we can apply equation 4.28 to find

$$\frac{\sum \lambda_j g_j}{\sqrt{\sum \dfrac{\lambda_j^2}{w_j}}} = \frac{8.39}{\sqrt{13.44}} = 2.29$$

as our Z value which is significant at p = .011 one-tailed.

The four effect sizes of this example were chosen to be the equivalents in units of g to the effect sizes of example 20 which were in units of r. The Z based on g is somewhat larger (by 14%) than the Z based on r (2.01) and the p of .011 is somewhat more significant than that for example 20 (p = .022). The agreement, therefore, is hardly perfect but it is close enough for practical purposes.

If a meta-analyst has a favorite effect size estimate, he or she need not fear that a different meta-analyst employing a different effect size estimate would reach a dramatically different conclusion. However, what should *not* be done is to employ a variety of effect size estimates, perform the various meta-analytic procedures on all of them and report only those results most pleasing to the meta-analyst. There is nothing wrong with employing multiple effect size estimates, but all analyses conducted should also be reported. General and special equations showing the relationships between g and r are given as equations 2.27, 2.28, 4.22, and 4.23.

If our effect size estimate were the difference between proportions (d′), our procedure would be analogous to that when our effect size estimate was Hedges's g. Once again we compute the reciprocal (w) of the estimated variance of d' $(1/w)$ for each study. We employ equation 4.6 when the individual sample sizes n_1 and n_2 are known and unequal and equation 4.7 when they are unknown or when they are equal. The equations are as follows:

$$w = \frac{n_1 n_2}{n_2 p_1 (1 - p_1) + n_1 p_2 (1 - p_2)} \qquad [4.6]$$

$$w = \frac{N}{1 - d'^2} \qquad [4.7]$$

Once we have w we can test any contrast by means of equation 4.28 (Rosenthal & Rubin, 1982a) but substituting d' for g:

$$\frac{\sum \lambda_j d'_j}{\sqrt{\sum \frac{\lambda_j^2}{w_j}}} \quad \text{is distributed approximately as } Z. \qquad [4.29]$$

In this application w_j is defined as in equations 4.6 or 4.7 and λ_j is as defined above.

Example 22. Studies A, B, C, and D yield effect sizes of $d' = .89, .76, .23,$ and $.59$, respectively, all with $N = 12$. As in example 21, we assume 8, 6, 4, and 2 hours of peer tutoring per month were employed in Studies A, B, C, and D, respectively. Again we want to test the linear contrast with λ's of 3, 1, -1, and -3. Table 4.7 lists the ingredients required to compute our test of significance (Z) for the contrast. Now we can apply equation 4.29 to find:

$$\frac{\sum \lambda_j d'_j}{\sqrt{\sum \frac{\lambda_j^2}{w_j}}} = \frac{1.43}{\sqrt{.7592}} = 1.64$$

as our Z value which is significant at $p = .050$ one-tailed.

TABLE 4.7
Work Table for Computing Contrasts Among Effect Sizes (d')

Study	N	d'	d'^2	$1-d'^2$	λ[a]	λ^2	$\lambda d'$	w_j[b]	$\frac{\lambda^2}{w}$
A	12	.89	.79	.21	3	9	2.67	57.14	.1575
B	12	.76	.58	.42	1	1	.76	28.57	.0350
C	12	.23	.05	.95	−1	1	−.23	12.63	.0792
D	12	.59	.35	.65	−3	9	−1.77	18.46	.4875
Σ	48	2.47	1.77	2.23	0	20	1.43	116.80	.7592

a. Determined by theory but with $\Sigma\lambda = 0$.

b. Obtainable from: $w = \dfrac{N}{1 - d'^2}$ (equation 4.7).

TABLE 4.8
Tests for Linear Contrasts in Effect Sizes Defined as r, g, and d'

	Effect Sizes		
	r	g	d'
Study A	.89	3.56	.89
Study B	.76	2.13	.76
Study C	.23	.43	.23
Study D	.59	1.33	.59
Median	.68	1.73	.68
Mean	.68[a]	1.86	.62
Z (linear contrast)	2.01	2.29	1.64
p	.022	.011	.050

a. Based on Fisher's z_r transformation.

The four effect sizes of this example were chosen to be equivalent in units of d' to the effect sizes of example 20 (r) and example 21 (g). Table 4.8 summarizes the data for the three effect size estimates of examples 20, 21, and 22. The three Z tests of significance of the linear contrast are somewhat variable, with the Z for the effect size estimator g being about 14% larger than that for r and the Z for the effect size estimator d' being about 18% smaller than that for r. However, the range of significance levels is not dramatic with the most significant result at $p = .011$ and the least significant at $p = .050$.

Before leaving the topic of focused tests, it should be noted that their use is more efficient than the more common procedure of counting each effect size or significance level as a single observation (e.g., Eagly & Carli, 1981; Hall, 1980; Rosenthal & Rubin, 1978; Smith et al., 1980). In that procedure we might, for example, compute a correlation between the Fisher z_r values and the λ's of example 20 to test the hypothesis of greater effect size being associated with greater contact time. Although that r is substantial (.77), it does not even approach significance because of the small number of df upon which the r is based. The procedures employing focused tests or contrasts employ much more of the information available and, therefore, are less likely to lead to Type II errors.

III.C. Combining Studies

III.C.1. Significance testing. After comparing the results of any set of three or more studies it is an easy matter also to combine the p levels of the set of studies to get an overall estimate of the probability that the set of p levels might have been obtained if the null hypothesis of no relationship between X and Y were true. Of the various methods available that will be described in the next chapter, we present here only the generalized version of the method presented earlier in our discussion of combining the results of two groups.

This method requires only that we obtain Z for each of our p levels, all of which should be given as one-tailed. Z's disagreeing in direction from the bulk of the findings are given negative signs. Then, the sum of the Z's divided by the square root of the number (K) of studies yields a new statistic distributed as Z. Recapping,

$$\frac{\sum Z_j}{\sqrt{K}} \text{ is distributed as Z} \qquad [4.30]$$

Should we want to do so, we could weight each of the Z's by its df, its estimated quality, or any other desired weights (Mosteller & Bush, 1954; Rosenthal, 1978, 1980).

The general procedure for weighting Z's is to multiply each Z by any desired weight (assigned before inspection of the data), add the weighted Z's, and divide the sum of the weighted Z's by the square root of the sum of the squared weights as follows:

$$\text{Weighted Z} = \frac{\sum w_j Z_j}{\sqrt{\sum w_j^2}} \qquad [4.31]$$

Example 24 will illustrate the application of this procedure.

Example 23. Studies A, B, C, and D yield one-tailed p values of .15, .05, .01, and .001, respectively. Study C, however, shows results opposite in direction from the results of the remaining studies. The four Z's associated with these four p's, then, are 1.04, 1.64, −2.33, and 3.09. From equation 4.30 we have

$$\frac{\sum Z_j}{\sqrt{K}} = \frac{(1.04) + (1.64) + (-2.33) + (3.09)}{\sqrt{4}} = 1.72$$

as our new Z value which has an associated p value of .043 one-tailed or .086 two-tailed. We would normally employ the one-tailed p value if we had correctly predicted the bulk of the findings but would employ the two-tailed p value if we had not. The combined p that we obtained in this example supports the results of the majority of the individual studies. However, even if these p values (.043 and .086) were more significant, we would want to be very cautious about drawing any simple overall conclusion because of the very great heterogeneity of the four p values we were combining. Example 15, which employed the same p values, showed that this heterogeneity was significant at p = .0013. It should be emphasized again, however, that this great heterogeneity of p values could be due to heterogeneity of effect sizes, heterogeneity of sample sizes, or both. To find out about the sources of heterogeneity, we would have to look carefully at the effect sizes and sample sizes of each of the studies involved.

Example 24. Studies A, B, C, and D are those of example 23 just above, but now we have decided to weight each study by the mean rating of internal validity assigned it by a panel of methodologists. These weights (w) were 2.4, 2.2, 3.1, and 3.8 for Studies A, B, C, and D, respectively. Employing equation 4.31 we find:

$$\text{Weighted } Z = \frac{\sum w_j Z_j}{\sqrt{\sum w_j^2}} = \frac{(2.4)(1.04) + (2.2)(1.64) + (3.1)(-2.33) + (3.8)(3.09)}{\sqrt{(2.4)^2 + (2.2)^2 + (3.1)^2 + (3.8)^2}}$$

$$= \frac{10.623}{\sqrt{34.65}} = 1.80$$

as the Z of the weighted combined results of Studies A, B, C, and D. The p value associated with this Z is .036 one-tailed or .072 two-tailed. In this example weighting by quality of research did not lead to a very different result than was obtained when weighting was not employed (example 23); in both cases $p \cong .04$ one-tailed. Actually, it might be more accurate to say for example 23 that weighting was equal with all w's = 1 than to say that no weighting was employed.

III.C.2. Effect size estimation. When we combine the results of three or more studies we are at least as interested in the combined estimate of the effect size as we are in the combined probability. We follow here our earlier procedure of considering r as our primary effect size estimator while recognizing that many other estimates are possible. For each of the three or more studies to be combined we compute r and the associated Fisher z_r and have

$$\frac{\sum z_r}{K} = \bar{z}_r \qquad\qquad [4.32]$$

as the Fisher $\bar{z}_r$ corresponding to our mean r (where K refers to the number of studies combined). We use a table of Fisher z_r to find the r associated with our mean z_r. Should we want to give greater weight to larger studies we could weight each z_r by its df, i.e., $N - 3$ (Snedecor & Cochran, 1967, 1980), by its estimated research quality, or by any other weights assigned before inspection of the data.

The weighted mean z_r is obtained as follows:

$$\text{Weighted } \overline{z}_r = \frac{\sum w_j z_{r_j}}{\sum w_j} \qquad [4.33]$$

Example 26 will illustrate the application of this procedure.

Example 25. Studies A, B, C, and D yield effect sizes of r = .70, .45, .10, and −.15, respectively. The Fisher z_r values corresponding to these r's are .87, .48, .10, and −.15, respectively. Then, from equation 4.32 we have

$$\frac{\sum z_r}{K} = \frac{(.87) + (.48) + (.10) + (-.15)}{4} = .32$$

as our mean Fisher z_r. From our table of Fisher z_r values we find a z_r of .32 to correspond to an r of .31. Just as in our earlier example of combined p levels, however, we would want to be very cautious in our interpretation of this combined effect size. If the r's we have just averaged were based on substantial sample sizes, as was the case in example 16, they would be significantly heterogeneous. Therefore averaging without special thought and comment would be inappropriate.

Example 26. Studies A, B, C, and D are those of example 25 just above but now we have decided to weight each study by a mean rating of ecological validity assigned to it by several experts. These weights were 1.7, 1.6, 3.1, and 2.5 for Studies A, B, C, and D, respectively. Employing equation 4.33 we find:

$$\text{Weighted } Z = \frac{\sum w_j z_{r_j}}{\sum w_j} = \frac{(1.7)(.87) + (1.6)(.48) + (3.1)(.10) + (2.5)(-.15)}{1.7 + 1.6 + 3.1 + 2.5}$$

$$= \frac{2.182}{8.90} = .24$$

as our mean Fisher z_r, which corresponds to an r of .24. In this example weighting by quality of research led to a somewhat smaller estimate of combined effect size than did equal weighting (.24 versus .31).

III.C.2.a. Other effect size estimates. Any other effect size, e.g., Cohen's d, Hedges's g, Glass's Δ, the difference between proportions (d') and so on can be combined with or without weighting just as we have shown for r. The only difference is that when we combine r's we typically transform them to

Fisher's z_r's before combining, while for most other effect size estimates we combine them directly without prior transformation.

EXERCISES

Six experiments were conducted to investigate the effects of a new treatment procedure. The following table shows the effect size (r) obtained in each study and the number of patients employed in each study (a positive r means the new treatment was better):

Study	Effect Size (r)	N
1	.64	43
2	.33	64
3	.03	39
4	.02	46
5	−.04	24
6	−.04	20

1. Compute the significance level for each of the above studies and give the Z associated with each significance level.

2. Give the weighted and the unweighted mean effect size for these six studies.

3. Give the significance level associated with each of the two mean effect sizes of question 2.

4. Report and interpret the results of a test of the heterogeneity of these six effect sizes.

5. Test the hypothesis that larger studies obtained larger effect sizes in this set of studies. Report the Z, p, and r derived from this contrast.

6. Convert the effect sizes given above to Cohen's d or Hedges's g. Then answer questions 1 to 5 for this new effect size estimate.

5

Combining Probabilities

Various methods for combining independent probabilities are described and compared. A warning is offered against the direct combining of the raw data of different studies. Finally, the problem of the "file drawer" is discussed in which studies with null results are unpublished and unretrievable by the meta-analyst.

I. GENERAL PROCEDURES

In the preceding chapter, some basic procedures that can be used to compare and to combine levels of significance and effect size estimates were presented. In addition to the basic procedures presented, there are various alternative methods available for combining probability levels that are especially useful under particular circumstances.

In this section on general procedures we summarize the major methods for combining the probabilities obtained from two or more studies testing essentially the same directional hypothesis. Although it is possible to do so, no consideration is given here to questions of combining results from studies in which the direction of the results cannot be made immediately apparent, as would be the case for F tests (employed in analysis of variance) with df > 1 for the numerator or for chi-square tests (of independence in contingency tables) with df > 1. Although this section is intended to be self-contained, it is not intended to serve as a summary of all the useful ideas on the topic at hand that are contained in the literature referenced. The seminal work of Mosteller and Bush (1954) is especially recommended. For a review of the relevant literature see Rosenthal (1978a).

I.A. The Basic Methods

Table 5.1 presents the results of a set of five illustrative studies. The first column of information about the studies lists the results of the t test. The

TABLE 5.1
Summary of Seven Methods for
Combining Probabilities of Independent Experiments

Study		t	df	*One-tail* p	*Effect* Size r	Z	$-2 \log_e p$
1		+1.19	40	.12	.18	+1.17	4.24
2		+2.39	60	.01	.29	+2.33	9.21
3		−0.60	10	.72	−.19	−0.58	0.66
4		+1.52	30	.07	.27	+1.48	5.32
5		+0.98	20	.17	.21	+0.95	3.54
Σ		+5.48	160	1.09	+.76	+5.35	22.97
	Mean	+1.10	32	.22	+.15	+1.07	4.59
	Median	+1.19	30	.12	+.21	+1.17	4.24

NOTES: The seven methods follow.

1. Method of Adding Logs:

$$\chi^2(df = 2N) = \Sigma - 2 \log_e p = 22.97$$

$$p = .011 \text{ one-tail} \qquad [5.1]$$

2. Method of Adding Probabilities (Applicable when Σp near unity or less):

$$P = \frac{(\Sigma p)^N}{N!} = \frac{(1.09)^5}{5!} = .013 \text{ one-tail} \qquad [5.2]$$

3. Method of Adding t's:

$$Z = \frac{\Sigma t}{\sqrt{\Sigma[df/(df - 2)]}} = \frac{5.48}{\sqrt{40/38 + 60/58 + 10/8 + 30/28 + 20/18}} \qquad [5.3]$$

$$= \frac{5.48}{\sqrt{5.5197}} = 2.33,$$

$$p = .01 \text{ one-tail.}$$

4. Method of Adding Z's:

$$Z = \frac{\Sigma Z}{\sqrt{N}} = \frac{5.35}{\sqrt{5}} = 2.39, \qquad [5.4]$$

$$p = .009 \text{ one-tail}$$

5. Method of Adding Weighted Z's:

$$Z = \frac{T}{\sigma_T} = \frac{df_1 Z_1 + df_2 Z_2 + \ldots + df_n Z_n}{\sqrt{df_1^2 + df_2^2 + \ldots + df_n^2}} \qquad [5.5]$$

$$= \frac{(40)(+1.17) + (60)(+2.33) + \ldots + (20)(+0.95)}{\sqrt{(40)^2 + (60)^2 + \ldots + (20)^2}}$$

$$= \frac{244.2}{\sqrt{6600}} = 3.01,$$

$$p = .0013 \text{ one-tail}$$

6. Method of Testing Mean p:

$$Z = (.50 - \bar{p})(\sqrt{12N})$$ [5.6]

$$= (.50 - .22)\sqrt{12(5)} = 2.17,$$

$$p = .015 \text{ one-tail}$$

7. Method of Testing Mean Z:

$$t = \frac{\Sigma Z/N}{\sqrt{S^2_{(Z)}/N}} = \frac{+1.07}{\sqrt{.22513}} = 2.26, \text{ df} = 4,$$ [5.7]

$$p < .05 \text{ one-tail}$$

or

$$F = \frac{(\Sigma Z)^2}{(N)S^2_{(Z)}} = 5.09, \text{ df} = 1, 4,$$

$$p < .05 \text{ one-tail}$$

sign preceding t gives the direction of the results; a positive sign means the difference is consistent with the bulk of the results, a negative sign means the difference is inconsistent. The second column records the df upon which each t was based.

The third column gives the one-tailed p associated with each t. It should be noted that one-tail p's are always less than .50 when the results are in the consistent direction, but they are always greater than .50 when the results are not consistent. For example, study 3 with a t of $-.60$ is tabulated with a one-tail p of .72. If the t had been in the consistent direction, i.e., $+.60$, the one-tail p would have been .28. It is important to note that it is the direction of difference which is found to occur on the average that is assigned the $+$ sign, and hence the lower one-tail p. The basic computations and results are identical whether we were very clever and predicted the net direction of effect or not clever at all and got it quite wrong. At the very end of our calculations, we can double the final overall level of significance if we want to make an allowance for not having predicted the net direction of effect.

The fourth column of the table gives the size of the effect defined in terms of the Pearson r.

The fifth column gives the standard normal deviate, or Z associated with each p value. The final column of our table lists the natural logarithms of the one-tail p's (of the third column of information) multiplied by -2. Each is a quantity distributed as χ^2 with 2 df and is an ingredient of the first method of combining p levels to be presented in this section (Fisher, 1932, 1938).

I.A.1. Adding logs. The last column of our table is really a list of χ^2 values. The sum of independent χ^2's is also distributed as χ^2 with df equal to the sum of the df's of the χ^2's added. Therefore, we need only add the five χ^2's of our table and look up this new χ^2 with $5 \times 2 = 10$ df. The results are given just below the row of medians of our table; $\chi^2 = 22.97$, which is associated with a p of .011, one-tail, when df = 10.

The method of adding logs, sometimes called the Fisher method, though frequently cited, suffers from the disadvantage that it can yield results that are inconsistent with such simple overall tests as the sign test of the null hypothesis of a 50:50 split (Siegel, 1956). Thus for a large number of studies, if the vast majority showed results in one direction, we could easily reject the null hypothesis by the sign test even if the consistent p values were not very much below .50. However, under these situations the Fisher method would not yield an overall significant p (Mosteller & Bush, 1954). Another problem with the Fisher method is that if two studies with equally and strongly significant results in opposite directions are obtained, the Fisher method supports the significance of either outcome! Thus p's of .001 for A > B and .001 for B > A combine to a p < .01 for A > B or B > A (Adcock, 1960). Despite these limitations, the Fisher method remains the best known and most discussed of all the methods of combining independent probabilities (see Rosenthal, 1978 for a review of the literature). Because of its limitations, however, routine use does not appear indicated.

I.A.2. Adding probabilities. A powerful method has been described by Edgington (1972a) in which the combined probability emerges when the sum of the observed p levels is raised to the power equivalent to the number of studies being combined (N) and divided by N!. Essentially, this formula gives the area of a right triangle when the results of two studies are being combined, the volume of a pyramid when the results of three studies are combined, and the n-dimensional generalization of this volume when more studies are involved. Our table shows the results to be equivalent to those obtained by the Fisher method for this set of data. The basic Edgington method is useful and ingenious but is limited to small sets of studies, since it requires that the sum of the p levels not exceed unity by very much. When the sum of the p levels does exceed unity, the overall p obtained tends to be too conservative unless special corrections are introduced.

I.A.3. Adding t's. A method that has none of the disadvantages of the preceding two methods was described by Winer (1971). Based on the result that the variance of the t distribution for any given df is $df/(df - 2)$, it requires adding the obtained t values and dividing that sum by the square root of the sum of the df's associated with the t's after each df has been divided by df − 2.

The result of the calculation is itself approximately a standard normal deviate that is associated with a particular probability level when each of the t's is based on df of 10 or so. When applied to the data of our table, the Winer method yields p = .01, one-tail, a result very close to the earlier two results. The limitation of this method is that it cannot be employed when the size of the samples for which t is computed becomes less than three, because that would involve dividing by zero or by a negative value. In addition, the method may not give such good approximations to the normal with df < 10 for each t.

I.A.4. Adding Z's. Perhaps the simplest of all, the Stouffer method described in the last chapter (Mosteller & Bush, 1954) asks us only to add the standard normal deviates (or Z's) associated with the p's obtained, and divide by the square root of the number of studies being combined (Adcock, 1960; Cochran, 1954; Stouffer, Suchman, DeVinney, Star, & Williams, 1949, p. 45). Each Z was a standard normal deviate under the null hypothesis. The variance of the sum of independent normal deviates is the sum of their variances. Here, this sum is equal to the number of studies, since each study has unit variance. Our table shows results for the Stouffer method that are very close to those obtained by the method of adding t's (Z = 2.39 vs. Z = 2.33).

I.A.5. Adding weighted Z's. Mosteller and Bush (1954) have suggested a technique that permits us to weight each standard normal deviate by the size of the sample on which it is based (or by its df), or by any other desirable positive weighting such as the elegance, internal validity, or real-life representativeness (ecological validity) of the individual study. The method, illustrated in the last chapter, requires us to add the products of our weights and Z's, and to divide this sum by the square root of the sum of the squared weights. Our table shows the results of the application of the weighted Stouffer method with df employed as weights. We note that the result is the lowest overall p we have seen. This is because, for the example, the lowest p levels are given the heaviest weighting because they are associated with the largest sample sizes and df. Lancaster (1961) has noted that when weighting is employed, the Z method is preferable to weighting applied to the Fisher method for reasons of computational convenience and because the final sum obtained is again a normal variable. Finally, for the very special case of just two studies, Zelen and Joel (1959) describe the choice of weights to minimize type II errors.

I.A.6. Testing the mean p. Edgington (1972b) has proposed a normal curve method to be used when there are four or more studies to be combined. The mean of the p's to be combined is subtracted from .50, and this quantity is multiplied by the square root of 12N, where N is the number of studies to be combined. (The presence of a 12 derives from the fact that the variance of the population of p values is 1/12, when the null hypothesis of no treatment effects is true.)

I.A.7. Testing the mean Z. In this modification of the Stouffer method, Mosteller and Bush (1954) first convert p levels to Z values. They then compute a t-test on the mean Z value obtained with the df for t equal to the number of Z values available minus one. Mosteller and Bush, however, advise against this procedure when there are fewer than five studies to be combined. That suggestion grows out of the low power of the t test when based on few observations. Our table illustrates this low power by showing that this method yields the largest combined p of any of the methods reviewed.

I.B. Additional Methods

I.B.1. Counting. When the number of studies to be combined grows large, a number of counting methods can be employed (Brozek & Tiede, 1952; Jones & Fiske, 1953; Wilkinson, 1951). The number of p values below .50 can be called $+$, the number of p values above .50 can be called $-$, and a sign test can be performed. If 12 of 15 results are consistent in either direction, the sign test tells us that results so rare "occur by chance" only 3.6 % of the time. This procedure, and the closely related one that follows, have been employed by Hall (1979).

The χ^2 statistic may also be useful in comparing the number of studies expected to reach a given level of significance under the null hypothesis with the number actually reaching that level (Rosenthal, 1969, 1976; Rosenthal & Rosnow, 1975; Rosenthal & Rubin, 1978a). In this application there are two cells in our table of counts, one for the number reaching some critical level of p, the other for the number not reaching that critical level of p. When there are 100 or more studies available, we can set our critical p level at .05. Our expected frequency for that cell is .05N while our expected frequency for the other cell is .95N. For example, suppose that 12 of 120 studies show results at $p \leq .05$ in the same direction. Then our expected frequencies for the two cells are .05(120) and .95(120) respectively, as shown in Table 5.2.

It is not necessary to set our critical value of p at .05. We could as well use .10 or .01. However, it is advisable to keep the expected frequency of our smaller cell at 5 or above. Therefore, we would not use a critical value of .01 unless we had at least 500 studies altogether. To keep our smaller expected frequency at 5 or more we would use a critical level of .10 if we had 50 studies, a critical level of .20 if we had 25 studies, and so on. More generally, when there are fewer than 100 studies but more than 9, we enter in one cell an expected frequency of 5 and in the other an expected frequency of $N-5$. The observed frequency for the first cell, then, is the number of studies reaching a

TABLE 5.2
Counting Method for Assessing Overall
Significance of a Relationship (χ^2 Method)

Counts	Studies Reaching $p \leq .05$	Studies Not Reaching $p \leq .05$	Σ
Obtained	12	108	120
Expected (if null hypothesis true)	6[a]	114[b]	120

NOTE: $\chi^2(1) = \Sigma \dfrac{(O - E)^2}{E} = \dfrac{(12 - 6)^2}{6} + \dfrac{(108 - 114)^2}{114} = 6.32, p = .012$ [5.8]

or, since $Z = \sqrt{\chi^2(1)}$, $Z = \sqrt{6.32} = 2.51, p = .006$, one-tailed.   [5.9]

a. Computed from $.05(N) = .05(120) = 6$.
b. Computed from $.95(N) = .95(120) = 114$.

$p < \frac{5}{N}$. The observed frequency for the second cell is the number of studies with $p > \frac{5}{N}$. The resulting χ^2 can then be entered into a table of critical χ^2 values. Alternatively, the square root of χ^2 can be computed to yield Z, the standard normal deviate. Although clear-cut results on the issue are not available, it appears likely that the counting methods are not as powerful as other methods described here.

I.B.2. Blocking. The last method, adapted from the procedure given by Snedecor and Cochran (1967; see also Cochran & Cox, 1957) requires that we reconstruct the means, sample sizes, and mean square within conditions for each of our studies. We then combine the data into an overall analysis of variance in which treatment condition is the main effect of primary interest and in which studies are regarded as a blocking variable. If required because of differences among the studies in their means and variances, the dependent variables of the studies can be put onto a common scale (e.g., zero mean and unit variance).

When studies are assumed to be a fixed factor, as they sometimes are (Cochran & Cox, 1957), or when the MS for treatments × studies is small relative to the MS within, the treatment effect is tested against the pooled MS within (Cochran & Cox, 1957). When the studies are regarded as a random factor and when the MS for treatments × studies is substantial relative to the MS within (say, $F > 2$), the treatments × studies effect is the appropriate error term for the treatment effect. Regardless of whether studies are viewed as fixed or random factors, the main effect of studies and the interaction of treatments × studies are tested against the MS within.

Substantial main effects of studies may or may not be of much interest, but substantial treatments × studies interaction effects will usually be of considerable interest. It will be instructive to study the residuals defining

TABLE 5.3
The Blocking Method of Combining Probabilities
Applied to the Studies of Table 5.1

Study	Control Mean	(n)	Experimental Mean	(n)	Mean	MS error
1	0.48	(21)	2.00	(21)	1.24	17.13
2	0.00	(31)	2.48	(31)	1.24	16.69
3	2.00	(6)	0.48	(6)	1.24	19.25
4	0.12	(16)	2.36	(16)	1.24	17.37
5	0.36	(11)	2.12	(11)	1.24	17.74
Mean	.592		1.888		1.24	17.64

Analysis of Variance: Unweighted Means				
Source	SS	df	MS	F
Treatments	4.1990	1	4.1990	2.98*
Studies	0.	4	0.[a]	—
Treatments x studies	5.2442	4	1.3110	—
Error		160	1.4110[b]	

a. In the example constructed here and, more generally, in cases wherein the data from each study are standardized with zero mean and unit variance, the mean square for studies is always zero, i.e., since the means of all studies have been set equal to each other (to zero) the between studies SS and MS must equal zero.
b. Computations are reviewed in the text.
*$Z = 1.70, p = .045$, one tail

the interaction closely for clues as to the nature of the possible moderating variables affecting the operation of the treatment effect. Analysis of the residuals might show, for example, that it is the better (or more poorly) designed studies that show greater predicted effects. The blocking method is sometimes not applicable because authors have not reported sufficient data in their papers.

Table 5.3 illustrates this last method as applied to the set of five studies we have been using as our example (see Table 5.1). An unweighted means analysis of variance was computed and the results fell within the range of results obtained by our earlier described methods. The only real disadvantage of this approach is that it may involve considerably more work than some of the other methods. This will be especially true when the number of studies grows from just a few to dozens, scores, or hundreds. The computations for the unweighted means analysis of variance are shown next.

I.B.2.a. Computations: unweighted means. The details of the unweighted means analysis of variance are given elsewhere (e.g., Rosenthal & Rosnow, 1984a, chapter 20). Basically, we perform our computations on the means of the control and experimental conditions of the five studies.

$$\text{Total SS} = \Sigma(M - \bar{M})^2 = (0.48 - 1.24)^2 + (2.00 - 1.24)^2 + \ldots +$$
$$(0.36 - 1.24)^2 + (2.12 - 1.24)^2 = 9.4432 \qquad [5.10]$$

$$\text{Row (Studies) SS} = \Sigma[c(M_R - \bar{M})^2] = 2(1.24 - 1.24)^2 + \ldots +$$
$$2(1.24 - 1.24)^2 = 0 \qquad [5.11]$$

$$\text{Column (Treatments) SS} = \Sigma[r(M_C - \bar{M})^2] = 5(.592 - 1.24)^2 +$$
$$5(1.888 - 1.24)^2 = 4.1990 \qquad [5.12]$$

$$\text{Row} \times \text{Column SS} = \text{Total SS} - \text{Row SS} - \text{Column SS}$$
$$= 9.4432 - 0 - 4.1990 = 5.2442 \qquad [5.13]$$

When divided by their appropriate df the Studies, Treatments, and Studies by Treatments SS's yield MS's of 0, 4.1990, and 1.3110, respectively.

The error term is obtained by dividing the MS error from the original one-way analysis of variance of the 10 conditions (17.64) by the harmonic mean of the sample sizes, n_h. In this case $n_h = 12.5016$ so our error term is

$$\frac{17.64}{12.5016} = 1.4110$$

as shown in Table 5.3.

I.C. Choosing a Method

Table 5.4 shows the advantages, limitations, and indications for use of each of the nine methods of combining probabilities. Various methods have special advantages under special circumstances. Suppose we were confronted by 200 studies, each provided with only the information that it did or did not reach a given alpha level. A counting method (χ^2) gives a very quick test, if not a very elegant or powerful estimate of overall probability. With so many studies to process we would probably decide against the blocking method on the grounds that the work required would not be justified by any special benefits. We would not be able to apply the basic method of adding probabilities for reasons given earlier. Most other methods are applicable, however.

If we were combining only a very few studies, we might favor the method of adding probabilities. We would avoid both the method of testing the mean Z and the counting methods, which do better on larger numbers of studies.

There is no best method under all conditions (Birnbaum, 1954), but the one that seems most serviceable under the largest range of conditions is that of adding Z's, with or without weighting. When the number of studies is small, it can be suggested that at least two other procedures also be employed and the overall p's emerging from all three be reported. When the number of studies is large, a useful combination would seem to be the

TABLE 5.4
Advantages and Limitations of Nine Methods
of Combining Probabilities

Method	Advantages	Limitations	Use When
1. Adding Logs	Well-established historically	Cumulates poorly; can support opposite conclusions.	N of studies small ($\leqslant 5$)
2. Adding p's	Good power	Inapplicable when N of studies (or p's) large unless complex corrections are introduced.	N of studies small ($\Sigma p \leqslant 1.0$)
3. Adding t's	Unaffected by N of studies given minimum df per study	Inapplicable when t's based on very few df.	Studies not based on too few df
4. Adding Z's	Routinely applicable; simple	Assumes unit variance when under some conditions Type I or Type II errors may be increased.	Anytime
5. Adding Weighted Z's	Routinely applicable, permits weighting	Assumes unit variance when under some conditions Type I or Type II errors may be increased.	Whenever weighting desired
6. Testing Mean p	Simple	N of studies should not be less than four.	N of studies $\geqslant 4$
7. Testing Mean Z	No assumption of unit variance	Low power when N of studies small.	N of studies $\geqslant 5$
8. Counting	Simple and robust	Large N of studies needed; may be low in power.	N of studies large
9. Blocking	Displays all means for inspection, thus facilitating search for *moderators* (variables altering the relationship between independent and dependent variables).	Laborious when N large; insufficient data may be available.	N of studies not too large

method of adding Z's combined with one or more of the counting methods as a check. Practical experience with the various methods suggests that there is only rarely a serious discrepancy among appropriately chosen methods. It goes without saying, of course, that any overall p that has been computed (or its associated test statistic with df) should be reported and not suppressed for being higher or lower than the investigator might like.

To make possible the computations described in this chapter, authors should routinely report the exact t, F, Z, or other test statistic along with its df or N, rather than simply making such vague statements as "t was significant at $p < .05$."

Reporting the test statistic along with an approximate p level also seems preferable to reporting the "exact" p level for three reasons: (1) the exact p level may be difficult to determine without a computer, (2) ambiguity about one-tail versus two-tail usage is avoided, and (3) the test statistic allows us to compute exact p as well as the effect size. Speaking of effect size, it would be highly desirable if editors routinely required the report of an effect size (e.g., r, g, Δ, or d) for every test statistic reported.

Finally, it should be noted that even if we have established a low combined p, we have said absolutely nothing about the typical size of the effect the "existence" of which we have been examining. We owe it to our readers to give for each combined p estimate an estimate of the probable size of the effect in terms of a correlation coefficient, a σ unit, or some other estimate. This estimated effect size should be accompanied, when possible, by a confidence interval.

I.D. On Not Combining Raw Data

Sometimes it happens that the raw data of two or more studies are available. We have seen how these data could be appropriately combined in the method of blocking. There may, however, be a temptation to combine the raw data without first blocking or subdividing the data on the basis of the studies producing the data. The purpose of this section is to help avoid that temptation by showing the very misleading or even paradoxical results that can occur when raw data are pooled without blocking.

Table 5.5 shows the results of four studies in which the correlation between variables X and Y is shown for two subjects. The number of subjects per study makes no difference and the small number (n = 2) is employed here only to keep the example simple. For each of the four studies the correlation (r) between X and Y is -1.00. However, no matter how we combine the raw data of these four studies, the correlation is never negative again. Indeed, the range of r's is from zero (as when we pool the data between any two adjacent studies) to .80 (as when we pool the data from studies 1 and 4). The remainder of Table 5.5 shows the six different correlations that are possible (.00, .45, .60, .67, .72, .80) as a function of which studies are pooled.

TABLE 5.5
Effects of Pooling Raw Data: Four Studies

	Study 1		Study 2		Study 3		Study 4	
	X	Y	X	Y	X	Y	X	Y
Subject 1	2	0	4	2	6	4	8	6
Subject 2	0	2	2	4	4	6	6	8
Mean	1.0	1.0	3.0	3.0	5.0	5.0	7.0	7.0
r	−1.00		−1.00		−1.00		−1.00	

Correlations obtained when pooling:		Two Studies			Three or Four Studies		
r =		.00	.60	.80	.45	.67	.72
Pooled studies:		1+2	1+3	1+4	1,2,3	1,2,3,4	1,2,4
		2+3	2+4		2,3,4		1,3,4
		3+4					

How can these anomalous results be explained? Examination of the means of the X and Y variables for the four studies of Table 5.5 helps us understand. The means of the X and Y variables differ substantially from study to study and are substantially positively correlated. Thus, in study 1 the X and Y scores (although perfectly negatively correlated) are all quite low relative to the X and Y scores of study 4 which are all quite high (although also perfectly negatively correlated). Thus, across these studies in which the variation is substantial, we have an overall positive correlation between variables X and Y. Within these studies, where the correlations are negative (−1.00) the variation in scores is relatively small, small enough to be swamped by the variation between studies.

Although there may be times when it is useful to array the data from multiple studies in order to see an overall pattern of results, or to see what might happen if we planned a single study with variation equivalent to that shown by a set of pooled studies, Table 5.5 serves as serious warning of how pooled raw data can lead to conclusions (though not necessarily "wrong") opposite to those obtained from individual, less variable studies.

I.D.1. Yule's or Simpson's Paradox. Over 80 years ago G. Udny Yule (1903) described a related problem in dealing with 2 × 2 tables of counts. He showed how two studies in which no relationship (r = .00) was found between the variables defined by the two rows and the two columns, could yield a positive correlation (r = .19) when the raw data were pooled. Similarly, Simpson (1951) showed how two studies with modest positive correlations (r's = .03 and .04) could yield a zero correlation when the raw data were pooled. Table 5.6 illustrates the problem described by Yule (1903), by Simpson (1951) and by others (e.g., Birch, 1963; Blyth, 1972; Fienberg, 1977; Glass et al., 1981; and Upton, 1978).

TABLE 5.6
Effects of Pooling Tables of Counts

	Study 1		Study 2		Pooled	
	Alive	Dead	Alive	Dead	Alive	Dead
Example I						
Treatment	100	1000	100	10	200	1010
Control	10	100	1000	100	1010	200
Σ	110	1100	1100	110	1210	1210
	r = 0		r = 0		r = .67	
Example II						
Treatment	50	100	50	0	100	100
Control	0	50	100	50	100	100
Σ	50	150	150	50	200	200
	r = .33		r = .33		r = 0	

In Example I of Table 5.6 we see two studies showing zero correlation between the treatment condition and the outcome. When the raw data of these two studies are pooled, however, we find a dramatic correlation of .67 suggesting that the treatment was harmful. Note that in Study 1 only 9% of patients survived, while 91% received the treatment, whereas in Study 2, 91% of patients survived but only 9% received the treatment. It is these inequalities of row and column totals that lead to Yule's (or Simpson's) Paradoxes.

Example II of Table 5.6 shows two studies each obtaining a strong effect favoring the treatment condition (r = .33). When these two studies were pooled, however, these strong effects vanished. Note that in Study 1 only 25% of patients survived while 75% received the treatment, whereas in Study 2, 75% of patients survived but only 25% received the treatment. Had row and column totals been equal, the paradoxes of pooling would not have occurred.

The moral of the pooling paradoxes is clear. Except for the exploratory purposes mentioned earlier, raw data should not be pooled without blocking. In most cases, effect sizes and significance levels should be computed separately for each study and only then combined.

II. SPECIAL ISSUES

Earlier in this chapter we saw that the method of adding Z's was perhaps the most generally serviceable method for combining probabilities. In the following section we provide procedures facilitating the use of this method.

II.A. Obtaining the Value of Z

The method of adding Z's requires that we begin by converting the obtained one-tailed p level of each study to its equivalent Z. The value of Z is zero when the one-tailed p is .50, positive as p decreases from p = .50 to p close to zero, and negative as p increases from .50 to p close to unity. Thus a one-tailed p of .01 has an associated Z of 2.33, while a one-tailed p of .99 has an associated Z of −2.33. These values can be located in the table of probabilities associated with observed values of Z in the normal distribution found in most textbooks on statistics.

Unfortunately for the meta-analyst, few studies report the Z associated with their obtained p. Worse still, the obtained p's are often given imprecisely as < .05 or < .01, so that p might be .001 or .0001 or .00001. If p is all that is given in a study, all we can do is use a table of the normal distribution to find the Z associated with a reported p. Thus, one-tailed p's of .05, .01, and .001 are found to have associated Z's of 1.65, 2.33, and 3.09, respectively. (If a result is simply called "nonsignificant," and if no further information is available, we have little choice but to treat the result as a p of .50, Z = 0.00.)

Since p's reported in research papers tend to be imprecisely reported we can do a better job of combining p's by going back to the original test statistics employed, e.g., t, F, or χ^2. Fortunately, many journals require that these statistics, along with their df, be reported routinely. The df for t and for the denominator of the F test in analysis of variance tell us about the size of the study. The df for χ^2 is analogous to the df for the numerator of the F test in analysis of variance and so tells us about the number of conditions, not the number of sampling units. Fortunately, the 1983 edition of the *Publication Manual of the American Psychological Association* has added a requirement that when reporting χ^2 test statistics the total N be given along with the df.

II.A.1. Test statistics. If a t test was employed, we can use a t table to find the Z associated with the obtained t. Suppose t(20) = 2.09 so that p = .025, one-tailed. We enter the t table at the row for df = 20 and read across to the t value of 2.09. Then we read down the column to the entry for df = ∞, which is the Z identical to the value of t with ∞ df (1.96). Suppose, however, that our t was 12.00 with 144 df. Even extended tables of t cannot help us when values of t are that large for substantial df (Federighi, 1959; Rosenthal & Rosnow, 1984a). A very accurate estimation of Z from t is available for such circumstances (Wallace, 1959):

$$Z = \sqrt{df \log_e (1 + \frac{t^2}{df})} \sqrt{1 - \frac{1}{2df}} \qquad [5.14]$$

A very useful and conservative approximation to this formula is also available (Rosenthal & Rubin, 1979a):

$$Z = t(1 - \frac{t^2}{4df})\qquad\qquad [5.15]$$

This approximation works best when $t^2 < df$; when $t^2 = df$, this approximation tends to be 10% smaller than the Z obtained from equation 5.14.

If the test statistic employed was F (from analysis of variance) and df for the numerator was unity, we take the $\sqrt{F}$ as t and proceed as we did in the case of t with df equal to the df of the denominator of the F ratio. We should note that F ratios of df > 1 in the numerator cannot be used in combining p levels to address a directional hypothesis.

If the test statistic employed was χ^2 (for independence in contingency tables) with df $= 1$, we take $\sqrt{\chi^2}$ directly, since $\chi^2(1) = Z^2$. We should note that χ^2's of df > 1 cannot be used in combining p levels to address a directional hypothesis.

When $\sqrt{F}$ or $\sqrt{\chi^2}$ is employed we must be sure that Z is given the appropriate sign to indicate the direction of the effect.

II.A.2. Effect size estimates. Sometimes we want to find Z for a study in which no test statistic is given (e.g., t, F, χ^2), but an effect size estimator such as r (including point biserial r and phi), g, Δ, or d is given along with a rough p level indicator such as p $< .05$. In those cases we can often get a serviceable direct approximation of Z by using the fact that $(phi)^2 = \chi^2(1)/N$ so that $N(phi)^2 = \chi^2(1)$ and $\sqrt{N}(phi) = \sqrt{\chi^2(1)} = Z$.

In the case of r or point biserial r, multiplying by $\sqrt{N}$ will yield a generally conservative approximation to Z. A more accurate value can be obtained by solving for t in the equation:

$$t = \frac{r}{\sqrt{1-r^2}} \times \sqrt{df} \quad \text{or,} \quad t = \frac{r}{\sqrt{1-r^2}} \times \sqrt{N-2}\qquad [2.3]$$

and then employing t to estimate Z as shown in equations 5.14 or 5.15.

We will not review here how to get t from the other effect size estimators but that information is found in equations 2.3 - 2.13 (Tables 2.1 and 2.2), 4.19, and 4.20.

II.B. The File Drawer Problem

Statisticians and behavioral researchers have long suspected that the studies published in the behavioral and social sciences are a biased sample of the studies that are actually carried out (Bakan, 1967; McNemar, 1960;

Smart, 1964; Sterling, 1959). The extreme view of this problem, the file drawer problem, is that the journals are filled with the 5% of the studies that show type I errors, while the file drawers back at the lab are filled with the 95% of the studies that show nonsignificant (e.g., p > .05) results (Rosenthal, 1979a).

In the past, there was very little we could do to assess the net effect of studies tucked away in file drawers that did not make the magic .05 level (Rosenthal & Gaito, 1963; 1964). Now, however, although no definitive solution to the problem is available, we can establish reasonable boundaries on the problem and estimate the degree of damage to any research conclusion that could be done by the file drawer problem. The fundamental idea in coping with the file drawer problem is simply to calculate the number of studies averaging null results that must be in the file drawers before the overall probability of a type I error can be just brought to any desired level of significance, say p = .05. This number of filed studies, or the tolerance for future null results, is then evaluated for whether such a tolerance level is small enough to threaten the overall conclusion drawn by the reviewer. If the overall level of significance of the research review will be brought down to the level of *just significant* by the addition of just a few more null results, the finding is not resistant to the file drawer threat.

II.B.1. Computation. To find the number (X) of new, filed, or unretrieved studies averaging null results required to bring the new overall p to any desired level, say, just significant at p = .05 (Z = 1.645), one simply writes:

$$1.645 = \frac{K\overline{Z}}{\sqrt{K + X}} \qquad [5.16]$$

where K is the number of studies combined and $\overline{Z}$ is the mean Z obtained for the K studies.

Rearrangement shows that

$$X = \frac{K[K\overline{Z}^2 - 2.706]}{2.706} \qquad [5.17]$$

An alternative formula that may be more convenient when the sum of the Z's (ΣZ) is given rather than the mean Z, is as follows:

$$X = \frac{(\Sigma Z)^2}{2.706} - K \qquad [5.18]$$

One method based on counting rather than adding Z's may be easier to compute and can be employed when exact p levels are not available, but it is probably less powerful. If X is the number of new studies required to bring the overall p to .50 (not to .05), s is the number of summarized studies significant at $p < .05$ and n is the number of summarized studies not significant at .05, then

$$X = 19s - n \qquad [5.19]$$

where 19 is the ratio of the total number of nonsignificant (at $p > .05$) results to the number of significant (at $p < .05$) results expected when the null hypothesis is true.

Another conservative alternative when exact p levels are not available is to set $Z = .00$ for any nonsignificant result and to set $Z = 1.645$ for any result significant at $p < .05$.

The equations above all assume that each of the K studies is independent of all other $K - 1$ studies, at least in the sense of employing different sampling units. There are other senses of independence, however; for example, we can think of two or more studies conducted in a given laboratory as less independent than two or more studies conducted in different laboratories. Such nonindependence can be assessed by such procedures as intraclass correlations. Whether nonindependence of this type serves to increase type I or type II errors appears to depend in part on the relative magnitude of the Z's obtained from the studies that are "correlated" or "too similar." If the correlated Z's are on the average as high as or higher than the grand mean Z corrected for nonindependence, the combined Z we compute treating all studies as independent will be too large, leading to an increase in type I errors. If the correlated Z's are on the average clearly low relative to the grand mean Z corrected for nonindependence, the combined Z we compute treating all studies as independent will tend to be too small, leading to an increase in type II errors.

II.B.2. Illustration. In 1969, 94 experiments examining the effects of interpersonal self-fulfilling prophecies were summarized (Rosenthal, 1969). The mean Z of these studies was 1.014, K was 94, and Z for the studies combined was:

$$\frac{\Sigma Z}{\sqrt{K}} = \frac{K\bar{Z}}{\sqrt{K}} = \frac{94(1.014)}{\sqrt{94}} = 9.83$$

How many new, filed, or unretrieved studies (X) would be required to bring this very large Z down to a barely significant level ($Z = 1.645$)? From equation 5.17 of the preceding section:

$$X = \frac{K[K\bar{Z}^2 - 2.706]}{2.706} = \frac{94[94(1.014)^2 - 2.706]}{2.706} = 3263$$

One finds that 3,263 studies averaging null results ($\bar{Z} = .00$) must be crammed into file drawers before one would conclude that the overall results were due to sampling bias in the studies summarized by the reviewer. In a more recent summary of the same area of research (Rosenthal & Rubin, 1978) the mean Z of 345 studies was 1.22, K was 345, and X was 65,123. Thus over 65,000 unreported studies averaging a null result would have to exist somewhere before the overall results could reasonably be ascribed to sampling bias.

II.B.3. Guidelines for a tolerance level. At the present time, no firm guidelines can be given as to what constitutes an unlikely number of unretrieved and/or unpublished studies. For some areas of research 100 or even 500 unpublished and unretrieved studies may be a plausible state of affairs while for others even 10 or 20 seems unlikely. Probably any rough and ready guide should be based partly on K so that as more studies are known it becomes more plausible that other studies in that area may be in those file drawers. Perhaps we could regard as robust to the file drawer problem any combined results for which the tolerance level (X) reaches $5 K + 10$. That seems a conservative but reasonable tolerance level; the 5 K portion suggests that it is unlikely that the file drawers have more than five times as many studies as the reviewer, and the $+10$ sets the minimum number of studies that could be filed away at 15 (when $K = 1$).

It appears that more and more reviewers of research literatures will be estimating average effect sizes and combined p's of the studies they summarize. It would be very helpful to readers if for each combined p they presented, reviewers also gave the tolerance for future null results associated with their overall significance level.

EXERCISES

1. For each of the six studies summarized in the exercises of Chapter 4 compute t, df, the one-tail p, the Z associated with each of these p's, and the quantity $-2 \log_e p$.

2. Combine the probabilities of the six studies using the methods of (a) adding logs, (b) adding p's, (c) adding t's, (d) adding Z's, (e) adding weighted Z's, (f) testing mean p, and (g) testing mean Z.

3. Assume, for the moment, that the seven combined p's computed for question 2 are independent. Perform a test of the heterogeneity of the seven obtained p levels and interpret the resulting statistic and its associated p level.

4. For the 50 studies you were able to retrieve for a meta-analysis, the mean standard normal deviate (Z) was .75 (associated with a one-tailed p of about .23). How many unretrieved studies averaging null results ($Z = .00$) must there be in the file drawers before the overall result would be brought to the brink of nonsignificance at $p = .05$?

5. Imagine that we had the raw data available for all six studies of the table given in the exercises of Chapter 4. Explain in prose and demonstrate by numerical example how it might happen that if we pooled the raw data of all six studies we might obtain results opposite in direction to those we found in the exercises of Chapters 4 and 5.

6

Illustrations of
Meta-Analytic Procedures

Based on the results of actual meta-analyses, illustrations are provided of a variety of meta-analytic procedures. Examples are drawn from research on nonverbal communication skills, the validity of the PONS test, the detection of deception, the effects of interpersonal expectancies, the effects of psychotherapy, and sex differences in cognitive performance.

In earlier chapters when various meta-analytic procedures were described they were often illustrated with hypothetical examples in order to keep the computational examples small and manageable. In the present chapter, we will illustrate various meta-analytic procedures with real-life meta-analytic examples. In principle it would be possible to illustrate almost every meta-analytic procedure described in this book for every meta-analysis we will be examining. For purposes of exposition, however, we will employ each meta-analytic example to illustrate a small number of principles and procedures.

I. DISPLAYING AND COMBINING EFFECT SIZES

DePaulo and Rosenthal (1979) conducted a meta-analysis of studies of the relationship between skill at decoding nonverbal cues and skill at encoding nonverbal cues. Table 6.1 is an updated summary of the results of 19 studies. The stem-and-leaf display and its statistical summary were encountered earlier (Tables 3.8 and 3.9) as useful ways of displaying the results of a meta-analysis. It is more informative for the eye to follow the stem-and-leaf display than simply to be told that the median r was .16 or that the mean r was .13.

The first five entries of the summary statistics require no explanation. The quantity $Q_3 - Q_1$ gives the range for the middle 50% of the effect sizes. The quantity .75 $(Q_3 - Q_1)$ estimates σ quite accurately when the

TABLE 6.1
Stem-and-Leaf Plot and Statistical Summary of Correlations
Between Encoding and Decoding Skill

Correlations (r's)		Summary Statistics	
Stem	Leaf	(Based on r, not on z_r)	
.6	3 5	Maximum	.65
.5	5	Quartile 3 (Q_3)	.29
.4		Median (Q_2)	.16
.3	2	Quartile 1 (Q_1)	.00
.2	0 0 1 8 9	Minimum	−.80
.1	6	$Q_3 - Q_1$	.29
.0	0 0 0 4 5 5 9	$\hat{\sigma}[.75(Q_3 - Q_1)]$	.22
−.0		S	.33
−.1		Mean	.13
−.2		N	19
−.3	6	Proportion positive sign[a]	.88
−.4			
−.5			
−.6			
−.7			
−.8	0		

a. Of those having signs.

distribution is normal and, therefore, is similar to S when the distribution is normal. In the data of Table 6.1, S is substantially larger than .75 ($Q_3 - Q_1$) suggesting that these effect sizes may not be normally distributed. If a more formal test of normality is required, the Kolmogorov-Smirnov test can be employed (Lilliefors, 1967; Rosenthal, 1968).

A stem-and-leaf plot and its statistical summary can, of course, be made for any type of effect size estimator. For example, Rosenthal and Rosnow (1975, p. 23) compared the rates of volunteering for behavioral research in general of females and males. Their stem-and-leaf display was of 51 such differences in volunteering rates, i.e., the effect size estimator d'. In that analysis the median d' was .11 with females volunteering more than males on the average. This direction of difference was found in 84% of the studies of volunteering for behavioral research in general.

II. COMBINING EFFECT SIZES
AND SIGNIFICANCE LEVELS

As part of the construct validation of the PONS test, an instrument designed to measure sensitivity to nonverbal cues, Rosenthal, Hall, DiMatteo, Rogers, and Archer (1979) conducted or located 22 studies in which the PONS test total score was correlated with judges' ratings of subjects' interpersonal or nonverbal sensitivity. Table 6.2 shows the results of the meta-

TABLE 6.2
Stem-and-Leaf Plot and Statistical Summary of
Validity Coefficients (r) for the PONS Test

Correlations (r's)		Summary Statistics	
Stem	Leaf	(Based on r, not z_r)	
.5	5	Maximum	.55
.4	5 6 9	Quartile 3 (Q_3)	.33
.3	1 2 3 4	Median (Q_2)	.22
.2	0 2 2 6 9	Quartile 1 (Q_1)	.05
.1	0 1 5	Minimum	−.35
.0	0* 1 6	$Q_3 - Q_1$	.28
−.0	4	$\hat{\sigma}[.75(Q_3 - Q_1)]$	.21
−.1	9	S	.22
−.2		Mean	.20
−.3	5	N	22
		Proportion positive sign	.86
		Z of proportion positive	3.41[a]
		Combined Stouffer Z	3.73[b]
		t test of mean Z	3.86[c]
		Correlation between r and Z	.86[d]

a. p = .0003
b. p = .0001
c. p = .0005
d. p = .0000002 from equation 2.3.
*This r has a positive sign.

analysis. The display includes all the elements of Table 6.1 relevant to combining effect sizes. In addition, however, three methods of combining probabilities were also employed and are summarized in the lower portion of the summary statistics.

The first method of combining probabilities listed is one of the counting methods. Under the null hypothesis we expect 50% of the correlation coefficients to have a positive sign. However, the present results show 86% of the studies to have a positive sign. Given that 19 of the 22 r's were positive when only 11 were expected to be positive under the null hypothesis, we can employ the binomial expansion to calculate how often we expect a result that extreme, or more extreme, if the null hypothesis were true. Alternatively, tables are available to help us find the desired p more readily (e.g., Siegel, 1956).

For most practical applications, however, we can employ a normal approximation to the binomial distribution that will work quite well even for modest sized samples:

$$Z = \frac{2P - N}{\sqrt{N}} \qquad [6.1]$$

where P is the number of positive effect sizes obtained and N is the number of positive plus negative effect sizes obtained. Note that unsigned effect sizes are excluded from this analysis.

For the data of Table 6.2, P = 19 and N = 22. Therefore:

$$Z = \frac{2P - N}{\sqrt{N}} = \frac{2(19) - 22}{\sqrt{22}} = 3.41, p = .0003 \text{ one-tailed}$$

In this case, if we had employed the more laborious binomial expansion the p value would have been .0004 instead. In using the Z test we assign Z a positive value if the direction of the effect is in the predicted direction and a negative value if the direction is not the predicted one.

Table 6.2 also gives the Z obtained employing Stouffer's method. In this meta-analysis, the sum of the 22 Z's was 17.48. Therefore from equation 5.4 we have

$$\frac{\Sigma Z}{\sqrt{N}} = \frac{17.48}{\sqrt{22}} = 3.73 \text{ as our obtained Z, with } p = .0001, \text{ one-tailed}$$

The third method of combining significance levels employed in Table 6.2 was the method of testing the mean Z. In this meta-analysis, the mean square for the 22 Z's was .93. Therefore, from equation 5.7 we have

$$t(21) = \frac{\Sigma Z/N}{\sqrt{S^2_{(Z)}/N}} = \frac{17.48/22}{\sqrt{.93/22}} = 3.86$$

which, with 21 df, is significant at p = .0005 one-tailed.

Finally, Table 6.2 reports the correlation between the 22 effect sizes (r's) and their degree of statistical significance (Z's). The r of .86 is very large and can be explained on the grounds of this set of validity studies being carried out on fairly similar sample sizes. From equation 2.2 we know that the relationship between Z and r depends more on the square root of N than on N itself. For the 22 studies of this meta-analysis, the $\sqrt{N}$ ranges from 2.4 to 9.3, with a median $\sqrt{N}$ of 4.4. Because there is a certain homogeneity of sample sizes employed in various areas of research, we have often found very substantial correlations between effect sizes and levels of statistical significance (Rosenthal & Rubin, 1978a). This is a useful result, since it sometimes happens that we have access only to significance levels but would like to be able to make some guesses about effect sizes for a given area of research. On the basis of this result it is likely that, typically, within a given research area, more significant results will also be larger in magnitude.

III. COMBINING EFFECT SIZES AND BLOCKING

In their meta-analytic work on the accuracy of the detection of deception, Zuckerman et al. (1981) were able to retrieve 72 results estimating the
degree of accuracy. The magnitude of the accuracy was defined by r and the
median of the 72 r's was .32. In these 72 results, subjects were provided
with various sources of information or cues to deception including cues
from the face, the body, ordinary recorded speech, content filtered speech
(tone of voice), and written transcription of what was said.

Table 6.3 shows the median r obtained (and the corresponding z_r) for
nine sources or channels of information or combinations of channels. The
overall median r of .32 convinced us that deception was detectable, but told
us little about which channels might provide the best sources of information
to permit detection of deception. It was to learn about the relative contribution to detection of deception of various channels that we blocked or subdivided the 72 results into the nine subtypes of Table 6.3.

A clearer picture of the relative contribution to the detection of deception of the three major channels of face, body, and speech can be obtained by
rearranging the first seven sources of Table 6.3 into the $2 \times 2 \times 2$ array of
z_r's shown in Table 6.4. One can get a quick picture of the relative contribution of these three channels and their combinations by performing an analysis of variance on just the eight means shown. Note that the entry for no face,
no body, no speech is .00, a theoretical value assuming that there can be no
accuracy when there is no information.

The lower half of Table 6.4 shows the analysis of variance of the eight z_r's
of the upper half. Note that no tests of significance have been done. Our purpose here is merely to get an overview of the relative magnitude of the sources

TABLE 6.3
Median Accuracy of Detecting Deception (r)
in Nine Samples of Studies

Sample	Source of Information	N of Studies	Median r	z_r
1	Face and body and speech	21	.33	.35
2	Face and body	6	.07	.07
3	Face and speech	9	.45	.48
4	Face	7	− .08	− .08
5	Body and speech	3	.55	.62
6	Body	4	.10	.10
7	Speech	12	.36	.38
8	Tone of voice	4	.06	.06
9	Transcript	6	.40	.42
	Median	6	.33	.35

TABLE 6.4
**Accuracy of Detecting Deception (z_r) for Eight Sources of Information
Arranged as a 2 × 2 × 2 Factorial Analysis of Variance**

	Speech		No Speech	
	Face	No Face	Face	No Face
Body	.35	.62	.07	.10
No body	.48	.38	−.08	.00[a]

Sources of Variance	MS[b]	Proportion of Total Variance
Face	.0098	.02
Body	.0162	.04
Speech	.3784	.86
Face × body	.0128	.03
Face × speech	.0005	.00
Body × speech	.0025	.00[c]
Face × body × speech	.0220	.05

a. Theoretical value
b. All df = 1; since no significance testing was employed, no estimation of any MS for error was undertaken.
c. More precisely, .0057.

TABLE 6.5
**Accuracy of Detecting Deception (z_r) for Four Sources of Information
Arranged as a 2 × 2 Factorial Analysis of Variance**

	Content	No Content
Tone	.38	.06
No tone	.42	.00[a]

Sources of Variance	MS[b]	Proportion of Total Variance
Content	.1369	.98
Tone	.0001	.00
Content × tone	.0025	.02

a. Theoretical value.
b. All df = 1.

of variance shown. The analysis shows very clearly that speech is far and away the most important source of cues for the detection of deception.

Once we have seen that speech is the major source of information relevant to deception detection, we may want to get some idea of what aspect of speech (e.g., tone versus content) may be most important in providing relevant cues. Fortunately, we can address this question by employing samples 7, 8, and 9 of Table 6.3. Table 6.5 arrays these data analogously to Table 6.4. Again the results are clear. Of the two components of speech that could be examined for their relative contribution to the detection of deception, it is content rather than tone that provides the bulk of the useful information.

To recap this section, we went from an overall estimate of accuracy based on 72 results to a subdivision of results that could shed light on questions of theoretical interest to us. By arranging the subdivisions of our meta-analysis, we were able to show the relative dominance of speech over visual cues and further, to show that within speech, content dominates tone as a source of cues to deception. Had we wanted more formal significance testing, we could have employed the methods of focused comparisons of Chapter 4. Later in this chapter, we provide additional illustrations of the use of such more formal comparisons.

IV. COMBINING EFFECT SIZES, BLOCKING, AND CONFIDENCE INTERVALS

In their meta-analysis of 345 studies of interpersonal expectancy effects, Rosenthal and Rubin (1978) subdivided the studies into eight areas in which such studies had been conducted. They employed a stratified random sampling procedure to estimate effect sizes (Cohen's d) and confidence intervals for each of the eight areas of research. Table 6.6 shows that the entire 95% confidence interval for the area of animal learning lies above the confidence intervals for the areas of reaction time and laboratory interviews. The effects of experimenters' expectancies on the performance of their animal subjects appears dependably greater than the effects of experimenters' expectancies on the reaction time and interview responses of their human subjects.

Table 6.6 also shows that the widest confidence interval is around the mean effect size of studies carried out in everyday contexts such as schools,

TABLE 6.6
Effects of Interpersonal Expectancy
Obtained in Eight Areas of Research

Research Area	N of Studies	$\bar{d}$	95% Confidence Intervals:[c]		Correlation Between d and Level of Significance (Z)
			From	To	
Reaction time	9	.17	.03	.31	.91
Inkblot tests	9	.84	−.06	1.74	.85
Animal learning	15	1.73	.97	2.49	.69
Laboratory interviews	29[a]	.14	−.36	.64	.89
Psychophysical judgments	23[a]	1.05	.49	1.61	.62
Learning and ability	34[a]	.54	−.13	1.21	.66
Person perception	119[a]	.55	.10	1.00	.69
Everyday situations	112[b]	.88	−.34	2.10	.46
Estimated mean		.70	.30	1.10	.72

a. Analyses were based on a stratified random sample of 15 studies.
b. Analyses were based on a stratified random sample of 20 studies.
c. Confidence intervals were based on the number of studies available (not on the number of subjects available).

clinics, and workplaces. Computing confidence intervals for our overall meta-analytic results and also our subdivided or blocked meta-analyses gives us a good indication of the likely value of effect sizes we might expect to find in the relevant population and subpopulations. Computational details when the meta-analysis involves stratified random sampling are given in Rosenthal and Rubin (1978). The last column of Table 6.6 shows that, for all eight research areas, there is a substantial correlation between effect size (d) and level of significance (Z).

V. COMPARING EFFECT SIZES:
AN EARLY COMPARISON

A much earlier meta-analysis of studies of interpersonal expectancy effects was conducted on 10 samples of experimenters who had stated before their research began the mean data they expected to obtain (Rosenthal, 1961, 1963). For each sample, then, the correlation was computed between the data the experimenters expected to obtain and the data the experimenters actually did obtain. It should be noted that each of these samples was homogenous with regard to expectations that had been experimentally induced. Therefore, the obtained correlations do not assess the effects of experimentally-induced expectancies but only individual differences in expectancies *after* experimenters had been given an expectancy. The range of expectancies held by experimenters was very much restricted because of the expectations that had been induced by the investigator.

Table 6.7 shows the correlations between expected and obtained data for the 10 samples of experimenters. The purpose of this analysis was to compare two subsets of the 10 samples. The first five samples (1-5) of Table 6.7 were obtained under ordinary conditions of data collection; the last five samples (6-10) were obtained under conditions of high reactance (Brehm, 1966). The latter samples of experimenters had been offered special incentives to obtain the data they had been led to expect or had been more explicitly instructed to bias the results of their research. The question was whether these "hyper-motivated" experimenters might show a higher or a lower correlation of their expected with their obtained data than the more ordinarily motivated (i.e., control) samples of experimenters.

The last column of Table 6.7 shows the contrast weights (λ's) required to test the question of whether the first five r's differ from the last five r's. From equation 4.27 we have that

$$Z = \frac{\Sigma \lambda_j z_{r_j}}{\sqrt{\Sigma \frac{\lambda_j^2}{w_j}}} = \frac{(1)(2.65) + (1)(.68) + \ldots + (-1)(-.32)}{\sqrt{\frac{(1)^2}{3} + \frac{(1)^2}{3} + \ldots + \frac{(-1)^2}{3}}} = \frac{5.39}{\sqrt{3.11}}$$

$$= 3.06, p = .0022 \text{ two-tail.}$$

TABLE 6.7
Correlations between Data Expected and
Data Obtained in 10 Samples of Experimenters

Sample	N of Experimenters	r	z_r	w [a]	λ
1	6	.99	2.65	3	1
2	6	.59	.68	3	1
3	6	.43	.46	3	1
4	6	.41	.44	3	1
5	12	.31	.32	9	1
6	6	.00	.00	3	-1
7	6	-.10	-.10	3	-1
8	6	-.21	-.21	3	-1
9	6	-.21	-.21	3	-1
10	6	-.31	-.32	3	-1
Σ	66	1.90	3.71	36	0

a. $N - 3$

For these 10 samples, therefore, experimenters exposed to greater reactance obtained significantly lower correlations between expected and obtained data.

When a specific contrast is to be tested, it is not necessary first to test for the heterogeneity of effect sizes, just as it is not necessary to compute an overall F test in the analysis of variance when a contrast has been planned (Rosenthal & Rosnow, 1984a). However, if we had wanted a test for the heterogeneity of these 10 effect sizes, here is how we would have done it. First, employing equation 4.16 we would have obtained the weighted mean z_r:

$$\overline{z}_r = \frac{\Sigma(N_j-3)z_{r_j}}{\Sigma(N_j-3)} = \frac{3(2.65) + 3(.68) + \ldots + 3(-.32)}{3 + 3 + \ldots + 3} = \frac{13.05}{36} = .36$$

a quantity required for use in equation 4.15, the χ^2 test for the heterogeneity of effect size estimates:

$$\Sigma(N_j-3)(z_{r_j}-\overline{z}_r)^2 = 3(2.65 - .36)^2 + 3(.68 - .36)^2 + \ldots + 3(-.32 - .36)^2 = 20.46$$
$$= \chi^2(K-1) = \chi^2(9), p < .02.$$

Thus, the 10 effect sizes differ significantly among themselves.

V.A. Some Useful (Probably Low Power) Alternatives

The procedure we employed for comparing the first 5 to the last 5 effect sizes of Table 6.7 used all of the information in our data. That is, it was able to make use of the actual size of the sample employed in each of the studies being summarized. In this section, we note briefly some procedures that treat each study as a single observation so that the same result would be obtained whether each study employed a sample size of 10, or 100, or 1,000.

As a first example, suppose we simply computed a t test comparing the mean z_r's of the first and last five studies of Table 6.7. That t would be 2.44, which, with 8 df, would be significant at $p < .05$ two-tailed. If each of the z_r's of Table 6.7 had been based on an N of 100, this t would be unaffected. However, equation 4.27, which we applied to these data, would continue to yield more and more significant results as our sample sizes per study increased.

As a second example we can apply the Mann-Whitney U test (Siegel, 1956). This test asks whether the bulk of one population is greater than the bulk of a second population. (For a general discussion of this test see Siegel [1956].) For the very special case we have for the data of Table 6.7, i.e., the case of completely nonoverlapping distributions, and equal n per sample (5 and 5 for these data), we can estimate Z from

$$\sqrt{\frac{3n^2}{2n + 1}} \qquad\qquad [6.2]$$

This estimate works well even for samples as small as the present ones. For our data $n_1 = n_2 = n = 5$, so we find Z as

$$Z = \sqrt{\frac{3n^2}{2n + 1}} = \sqrt{\frac{3(5)^2}{2(5) + 1}} = 2.61, p = .009$$

two-tailed. Employing Siegel's more precise tables yields a two-tailed p of .008, a result that agrees very well with that of our approximation.

The use of these two methods is not recommended as a substitute for equation 4.27. However, they are useful for a quick preliminary view of the difference between two samples of studies. In addition to the disadvantage that these methods cannot profit from increasing n's per study, they also do not have the flexibility of equation 4.27 in permitting *any* kind of comparison one might wish to make.

VI. COMPARING EFFECT SIZES:
MORE RECENT COMPARISONS

For our final and most comprehensive meta-analytic illustration, we consider a "tertiary" analysis. The analysis will be of a re-analysis by Prioleau, Murdock, and Brody (1983) of the seminal meta-analysis by Smith et al. (1980). In general terms, the re-analysis by Prioleau et al., as well as an earlier re-analysis by Landman and Dawes (1982) support the conclusions drawn by Smith et al. (1980).

Prioleau et al. (1983) examined a subset of studies comparing the effects of psychotherapy to the effects of placebo treatments. In what follows we examine this subset of studies within the framework of meta-analytic procedures described in this book and as presented elsewhere recently (Rosenthal, 1983b).

Table 6.8 summarizes the result of the present meta-analysis. The 32 studies were divided (or blocked) into five groups. The first three groups were entirely comprised of students divided on the basis of age level into elementary, secondary, and college level. The last two groups were entirely comprised of patients divided on the basis of the type of placebo employed—psychological versus medical. The psychological placebo patients (as well as all the student groups) were those who received some form of placebo that could have been viewed by patients as psychological in some sense. The medical placebo patients were those who received only a pill placebo, i.e., they received only a "medical" placebo treatment.

The first two rows of Table 6.8 show the number of studies summarized and the total number of persons whose data entered into a determination of the average size of the effect (Hedges's g). The third row gives the mean g for each group, the fourth and fifth rows give the standard normal deviate (Z) and the p level associated with each mean g. The college students and the patients who, like the college students, were given psychological placebos both showed substantial benefits of psychotherapy relative to placebo controls and these differences were significant at p well less than .001. The grand mean effect size of .24 (p < .000005, one-tailed) was smaller than that obtained by Prioleau et al. and by Smith et al. because it was computed with weighting inversely as the variance of g as shown in equations 4.18 and 4.3.

Rows 6, 7, and 8 of Table 6.8 give the results of tests of heterogeneity of effect sizes, i.e., tests of whether the g's in each set of studies differ significantly among themselves. Studies of elementary school children and of patients receiving psychological placebo yielded g's that were significantly heterogeneous. (See equations 4.17 and 4.18.)

Lines 9, 10, and 11 address the question of the relationship between the size of the study and the size of the g. The Z's and p's for linear contrasts show that among elementary school children larger g's were found in smaller studies (p < .000005; r = -.24), but among patients receiving psychological placebos, larger g's were found in larger studies (p = .009; r = .16). Thus, although for all studies combined, larger g's are associated with smaller studies, there are statistically significant reversals of this overall relationship.

Table 6.9 shows that the mean g's of the five groups examined can be compared meaningfully within the framework of a set of four contrasts employing equations 4.28 and either 4.3 or 4.21. The first contrast shows that there is little difference between students and patients in the degree to which psychotherapy is more effective than placebo. The second contrast

TABLE 6.8
Summary of Statistics Employed in Meta-Analysis of Psychotherapy Effects

	Students			Patients		All Results Combined	Combined Results Reported in Prioleau et al. (1983)
	Elementary School	Secondary School	College Level	Psychological Placebo	Medical Placebo		
(1) Number of studies	6	6	10	6	4	32	32
(2) Total number of persons	363	306	319	236	216	1440	Not reported
(3) Weighted mean g	.17	.06	.53	.44	.02	.24[a]	.42 (unweighted)
(4) Z for mean g	1.58	0.52	4.56	3.26	0.15	4.50[b]	Not tested
(5) p for Z above[c]	.06	.30	.001	.001	.44	.001[d]	Not reported
(6) χ^2 for heterogeneity of g's	44.4	1.94	13.9	19.4	1.02	80.66	Not tested
(7) df for χ^2 above	5	5	9	5	3	27	Not reported
(8) p for χ^2 above	.001	.90	.15	.002	.80	.001	Not reported
(9) Z for linear contrast	-4.54	-0.57	-0.13	2.35	-0.91	-1.70	Not tested by contrasts
(10) p for Z above[c]	.001[d]	.28	.45	.009	.18	.04	Reported as n.s.
(11) r based on linear contrast	-.24	-.03	-.01	.16	-.06	-.05[e]	-.21

a. The five g's upon which this weighted mean is based differ significantly among themselves; $\chi^2(4) \cong 13.87$, $p < .01$.
b. Computed as $\Sigma Z/\sqrt{5}$.
c. One-tailed.
d. More precisely, $p < .000005$.
e. The five r's upon which this weighted mean r is based differ significantly among themselves; $\chi^2(4) \cong 22.75$, $p < .001$.

TABLE 6.9
Contrasts Among Five Groups of Studies
of Psychotherapy Effects

Contrast	Z	p (one-tailed)
Students versus patients	.20	.42
Linear trend in age of students	2.27	.012
Quadratic trend in age of students	2.08	.019
Psychological versus medical placebo	2.18	.015

shows that with increasing age of students, greater g's are obtained. The third contrast shows that the average of the elementary and college student groups yields a larger g than does the group of secondary students. (In interpreting these contrasts in age we should note that age is likely to be confounded here with such variables as IQ, type of treatment, type of placebo control, and so forth.) The fourth contrast shows that psychotherapy is more effective relative to psychological than to medical placebo controls. Perhaps pill placebos are so effective that it is difficult for psychotherapy to be superior to them.

To address this last question, to help understand the significant linear and quadratic contrasts in age, the meaning of the sometimes positive, sometimes negative correlation between g and N, and the significant heterogeneity of g's found among studies of elementary school children and studies of patients given psychological placebo, additional studies will be required.

This section was designed to illustrate how the systematic application of various meta-analytic procedures can lead to firmer inferences about a domain of research. At the same time, however, it should be clear that metaanalyses need not close off further research in an area. Indeed, they may be employed to help us formulate more clearly just what that research should be.

A similar set of meta-analytic procedures was recently carried out in the research area of sex differences in cognitive functioning (Rosenthal & Rubin, 1982b). In that analysis, we showed that, in the four areas of cognitive functioning investigated by Hyde (1981), effect sizes were significantly heterogenous. In addition, we showed that in all four areas, studies conducted more recently showed a substantial gain in cognitive performance by females relative to males (unweighted mean r = .40).

7

The Evaluation of Meta-Analytic
Procedures and Meta-Analytic Results

Criticisms of the meta-analytic enterprise are described and discussed under the general headings of sampling bias, information loss, problems of heterogeneity of method and of quality, problems of independence, exaggeration of significance levels, and the practical importance of any particular estimated effect size.

We have had an opportunity to examine a variety of meta-analytic procedures so that we would now be able to carry out meta-analyses of research areas. But should we want to? The purposes of this final chapter are to examine some negative evaluations of meta-analysis and to evaluate the merits of these evaluations.

In the years 1980, 1981, and 1982 alone, well over 300 papers have been published on the topic of meta-analysis (Lamb & Whitla, 1983). Does this represent a giant stride forward in the development of the behavioral and social sciences or does it signal a lemming-like flight to disaster? Judging by the reactions to past meta-analytic enterprises, there are some who take the more pessimistic view. Some three dozen scholars were invited to respond to the meta-analysis of studies of interpersonal expectancy effects (Rosenthal & Rubin, 1978). Although much of the commentary dealt with the substantive topic of interpersonal expectancy effects, a good deal of it dealt with methodological aspects of meta-analytic procedures and products. Some of the criticisms offered were accurately anticipated by Glass (1978) who had earlier received commentary on his meta-analytic work (Glass, 1976) and that of his colleagues (Smith & Glass, 1977; Glass et al., 1981). In this chapter, the criticisms of our commentators are grouped into a half-dozen conceptual categories, described, and discussed.

I. SAMPLING BIAS AND THE
FILE DRAWER PROBLEM

This criticism holds that there is a retrievability bias such that studies retrieved do not reflect the population of studies conducted. One version of this criticism is that the probability of publication is increased by the statistical significance of the results so that published studies may not be representative of the studies conducted. This criticism is well taken although it applies equally to traditional narrative reviews of the literature. One set of procedures that can be employed to address this problem was described in Chapter 5 when the file drawer problem was discussed.

A bizarre version of this criticism simply holds that the unretrieved studies are essentially a mirror image of the retrieved studies (Rosenthal & Rubin, 1978). Thus if the combined Z for 100 studies is $+6.50$, there is postulated to be, in the file drawers, another set of studies with combined $Z = -6.50$! No mechanism whereby this phenomenon may operate has been proposed and no reply to this criticism seems possible. One can too easily postulate a universe in which for every observed outcome there is an unobserved outcome equal and opposite in magnitude and/or in significance level.

II. LOSS OF INFORMATION

II.A. Overemphasis on Single Values

The first of two criticisms relevant to information loss notes the danger of trying to summarize a research domain by a single value such as a mean effect size. This criticism holds that defining a relation in nature by a single value leads to overlooking moderator variables. The force of this criticism is removed when meta-analysis is seen as including not only combining effect sizes (and significance levels) but also comparing effect sizes in both diffuse and, especially, in focused fashion.

II.A.1. Overlooking negative instances. A special case of the criticism under discussion is that, by emphasizing average values, negative cases are overlooked. There are several ways in which negative cases can be defined; e.g., $p > .05$, $r = 0$, r negative, r significantly negative, and so on. However we may define negative cases, when we divide the sample of studies into negative and positive cases we have merely dichotomized an underlying continuum of effect sizes or significance levels and accounting for negative cases is simply a special case of finding moderator variables.

II.B. Glossing Over Details

Although it is accurate to say that meta-analyses gloss over details, it is equally accurate to say that traditional narrative reviews do so and that data analysts do so in every study in which any statistics are computed. To summarize means to gloss over details. If we describe a nearly normal distribution of scores by the mean and σ we have nearly described the distribution perfectly. If the distribution is quadrimodal, the mean and σ will not do a good job of summarizing the data. It is the data analyst's job in the individual study, and the meta-analyst's job in meta-analysis, to "gloss well." Providing the reader with all the raw data of all the studies summarized avoids this criticism but serves no useful review function. Providing the reader with a stem-and-leaf display of the effect sizes obtained, along with the results of the diffuse and focused comparisons of effect sizes, does some glossing but it does a lot of informing besides.

There is, of course, nothing to prevent the meta-analyst from reading each study as carefully and assessing it as creatively as might be done by a more traditional reviewer of a literature. Indeed, we have something of an operational check on reading articles carefully in the case of meta-analysis. If we do not read the results carefully, we cannot obtain effect sizes and significance levels. In traditional reviews results may have been read carefully or not read at all with the abstract or the discussion section providing "the results" to the more traditional reviewer.

III. PROBLEMS OF HETEROGENEITY

III.A. Heterogeneity of Method

The first of two criticisms relevant to problems of heterogeneity notes that meta-analyses average over studies in which the independent variables, the dependent variables, and the sampling units are not uniform. How can we speak of interpersonal expectancy effects, meta-analytically, when some of the independent variables are operationalized by telling experimenters that tasks are easy versus hard or by telling experimenters that subjects are good versus poor task performers? How can we speak meta-analytically of these expectancy effects when sometimes the dependent variables are reaction times, sometimes IQ test scores, and sometimes responses to inkblots? How can we speak of these effects when sometimes the sampling units are rats, sometimes college sophomores, sometimes patients, sometimes pupils? Are these not all vastly different phenomena? How can they be pooled together in a single meta-analysis?

Glass (1978) has eloquently addressed this issue—the apples and oranges issue. They are good things to mix, he wrote, when we are trying to generalize to fruit. Indeed, if we are willing to generalize over subjects within studies, why should we not be willing to generalize over studies? If subjects behave very differently within studies we block on subject characteristics to help us understand why. If studies yield very different results from each other, we block on study characteristics to help us understand why. It is very useful to be able to make general statements about fruit. If, in addition, it is also useful to make general statements about apples, about oranges, and about the differences between them, there is nothing in meta-analytic procedures to prevent us from doing so. Indeed, Chapter 4 especially deals with these procedures in detail.

III.B. Heterogeneity of Quality

One of the most frequent criticisms of meta-analyses is that bad studies are thrown in with good. This criticism must be broken down into two questions: (1) What is a bad study? and (2) What shall we do about bad studies?

III.B.1. Defining "bad" studies. Too often, deciding what is a bad study is a procedure unusually susceptible to bias or to claims of bias (Fiske, 1978). Bad studies are too often those whose results we do not like or, as Glass et al. (1981) have put it, the studies of our "enemies." Therefore when reviewers of research tell us they have omitted the bad studies, we should satisfy ourselves that this has been done by criteria we find acceptable. A discussion of these criteria (and the computation of their reliability) can be found in Chapter 3.

III.B.2. Dealing with bad studies. The distribution of studies on a dimension of quality is of course not really dichotomous (good versus bad) but continuous with all possible degrees of quality. Because we dealt with the issue in detail in Chapter 3, we can be brief here: The fundamental method of coping with bad studies or, more accurately, variations in the quality of research, is by differential weighting of studies. Dropping studies is merely the special case of zero weighting.

The most important question to ask about study quality is asked by Glass (1976): Is there a relationship between quality of research and effect size obtained? If there is not, the inclusion of poorer quality studies will have no effect on the estimate of the average effect size though it will help to decrease the size of the confidence interval around that mean. If there *is* a relationship between the quality of research and effect size obtained, we can employ whatever weighting system we find reasonable (and that we can persuade our colleagues and critics also to find reasonable).

IV. PROBLEMS OF INDEPENDENCE

IV.A. Responses within Studies

The first of two criticisms relevant to problems of independence notes that several effect size estimates and several tests of significance may be generated by the same subjects within each study. This can be a very apt criticism under some conditions. Chapter 2 deals with the problem in detail.

IV.B. Studies within Sets of Studies

Even when all studies yield only a single effect size estimate and level of significance and even when all studies employ sampling units that do not also appear in other studies, there is a sense in which results may be non-independent. That is, studies conducted in the same laboratory, or by the same research group, may be more similar to each other (in the sense of an intraclass correlation) than they are to studies conducted in other laboratories or by other research groups (Jung, 1978; Rosenthal, 1966, 1969, 1979; Rosenthal & Rosnow, 1984c). The conceptual and statistical implications of this problem are not yet worked out. However, there are some preliminary data bearing on this issue that are at least moderately reassuring.

Table 7.1 shows a series of 94 studies blocked or subdivided into seven areas of research on interpersonal expectancy effects (Rosenthal, 1969). For each area, the combined Z was computed; once based on the n of studies in that area, and once based on the n of laboratories or principal investigators. For most of the research areas there is little difference in n between studies and laboratories so there is little difference in their Z's. The only noticeable difference in Z's is for the research area in which there were substantially more studies (n = 57) than there were laboratories (n = 20). Even there, however, it seems unlikely that we would have drawn very different conclusions from these two methods of analysis.

Perhaps the most important result, however, is seen when we compare the overall Z for all 94 studies with the overall Z for the 48 laboratories. There is less than a 3% decrease in the combined Z when we go from the analysis per study to the analysis per laboratory. It would be useful if similar analyses employing effect size estimates were available.

TABLE 7.1
Significance Levels Computed Separately
for Studies and for Laboratories

| | Studies | | Laboratories | | Difference |
Research Area	Z	n	Z	n	in Z's
Animal learning	8.64	9	8.46	5	.18
Learning and ability	3.01	9	2.96	8	.05
Psychophysical judgments	2.55	9	2.45	6	.10
Reaction time	1.93	3	1.93	3	.00
Inkblot tests	3.55	4	3.25	3	.30
Laboratory interviews	5.30	6	5.30	6	.00
Person perception	4.07	57	2.77	20	1.30
All studies	9.82	94[a]	9.55	48[a]	.27

a. Three entries were nonindependent and the mean Z across areas was used for the single independent entry.

V. EXAGGERATION OF SIGNIFICANCE LEVELS

V.A. Truncating Significance Levels

It has been suggested that all p levels less than .01 (Z values greater than 2.33) be reported as .01 (Z = 2.33) because p's less than .01 are likely to be in error (Elashoff, 1978). This truncating of Z's cannot be recommended and will, in the long run, lead to serious errors of inference (Rosenthal & Rubin, 1978). If there is reason to suspect that a given p level < .01 is in error it should, of course, be corrected before employing it in the meta-analysis. It should not, however, be changed to p = .01 simply because it is less than .01.

V.B. Too Many Studies

It has been noted as a criticism of meta-analyses that as the number of studies increases, there is a greater and greater probability of rejecting the null hypothesis (Mayo, 1978). When the null hypothesis is false and, therefore, ought to be rejected, it is indeed true that adding observations (either sampling units within studies or new studies) increases statistical power. However, it is hard to accept as a legitimate criticism of a procedure, a characteristic that increases its accuracy and decreases its error rate—in this case, type II errors. When the null hypothesis is really true, of course, adding studies does not lead to increased probability of rejecting the null hypothesis. Adding studies, it should also be noted, does not increase the size of the estimated effect.

A related feature of meta-analysis is that it may, in general, lead to a decrease in type II errors even when the number of studies is modest. The empirical support for this was described in Chapter 1 when the research by Cooper and Rosenthal (1980) was summarized. Procedures requiring the research reviewer to be more systematic and to use more of the information in the data seem to be associated with increases in power, i.e., decreases in type II errors.

VI. THE PRACTICAL IMPORTANCE OF
THE ESTIMATED EFFECT SIZE

Mayo (1978) criticized Cohen (1977) for calling an effect size large (d = .80) when it accounted for "only" 14% of the variance. Similarly, Rimland (1979) felt that the Smith and Glass (1977) meta-analysis of psychotherapy outcome studies sounded the death knell for psychotherapy because the effect size was equivalent to an r of .32 accounting for "only" 10% of the variance.

VI.A. The Binomial Effect Size Display (BESD)

Despite the growing awareness of the importance of estimating effect sizes, there is a problem in evaluating various effect size estimators from the point of view of practical usefulness (Cooper, 1981). Rosenthal and Rubin (1979b, 1982c) found that neither experienced behavioral researchers nor experienced statisticians had a good intuitive feel for the practical meaning of such common effect size estimators as r^2, omega^2, epsilon^2, and similar estimates.

Accordingly, Rosenthal and Rubin introduced an intuitively appealing general purpose effect size display whose interpretation is perfectly transparent: the binomial effect size display (BESD). There is no sense in which they claim to have resolved the differences and controversies surrounding the use of various effect size estimators but their display is useful because it is easily understood by researchers, students, and lay persons, applicable in a wide variety of contexts, and conveniently computed.

The question addressed by BESD is: what is the effect on the success rate (e.g., survival rate, cure rate, improvement rate, selection rate, and so on) of the institution of a new treatment procedure, a new selection device, or a new predictor variable? It therefore displays the change in success rate (e.g., survival rate, cure rate, improvement rate, accuracy rate, selection rate, etc.) attributable to the new treatment procedure, new selection device, or new predictor variable. An example shows the appeal of the display. Suppose the estimated mean effect size were found to be an r of .32, approximately the size of the effects reported by Smith and Glass (1977) and by Rosenthal and Rubin (1978) for the effects of psychotherapy and of interpersonal expectancy effects, respectively.

Table 7.2 is the BESD corresponding to an r of .32 or an r^2 of .10. The table shows clearly that it is absurd to label as modest an effect size equivalent to increasing the success rate from 34% to 66% (e.g., reducing a death rate from 66% to 34%). Even so small an r as .20, accounting for "only" 4% of the variance is associated with an increase in success rate from 40% to 60%, e.g., a decrease in death rate from 60% to 40%, hardly a trivial effect. It might be thought that the BESD can be employed only for dichotomous outcomes (e.g., alive vs. dead) and not for continuous outcomes (e.g., scores on a Likert-type scale of improvement due to psychotherapy, or gains in performance due to favorable interpersonal expectations). Fortunately,

TABLE 7.2
The Binomial Effect Size Display (BESD) for an r of .32
that Accounts for "Only" 10% of the Variance

| | Treatment Result | | |
Condition	Alive	Dead	Σ
Treatment	66	34	100
Control	34	66	100
Σ	100	100	200

TABLE 7.3
Changes in Success Rates (BESD)
Corresponding to Various Values of r² and r

Effect Sizes		Equivalent to a Success Rate Increase		Difference in
r^2	r	From	To	Success Rates[a]
.00	.02	.49	.51	.02
.00	.04	.48	.52	.04
.00	.06	.47	.53	.06
.01	.08	.46	.54	.08
.01	.10	.45	.55	.10
.01	.12	.44	.56	.12
.03	.16	.42	.58	.16
.04	.20	.40	.60	.20
.06	.24	.38	.62	.24
.09	.30	.35	.65	.30
.16	.40	.30	.70	.40
.25	.50	.25	.75	.50
.36	.60	.20	.80	.60
.49	.70	.15	.85	.70
.64	.80	.10	.90	.80
.81	.90	.05	.95	.90
1.00	1.00	.00	1.00	1.00

a. The difference in success rates in a BESD is identical to r.

however, the BESD works well for both types of outcomes under a wide variety of conditions (Rosenthal & Rubin, 1982c).

A great convenience of the BESD is how easily we can convert it to r (or r^2) and how easily we can go from r (or r^2) to the display.

Table 7.3 shows systematically the increase in success rates associated with various values of r^2 and r. For example, an r of .30, accounting for "only" 9% of the variance is associated with a reduction in death rate from 65% to 35%, or more generally with an increase in success rate from 35% to 65%. The last column of Table 7.3 shows that the difference in success rates is identical to r. Consequently, the experimental group success rate in the BESD is computed as .50 + r/2 whereas the control group success rate is computed as .50 − r/2.

VI.B. The Propranolol Study and the BESD

On October 29, 1981, the National Heart, Lung, and Blood Institute officially discontinued its placebo-controlled study of propranolol because the results were so favorable to the treatment that it would be unethical to keep the placebo control patients from receiving the treatment (Kolata, 1981). The two-year data for this study were based on 2108 patients and $\chi^2(1)$ was approximately 4.2. What then, was the size of the effect that led the Institute to break off its study? Was the use of propranolol accounting for 90% of the variance in death rates? Was it 50% or 10%, the overly modest effect size that should prompt us to give up psychotherapy? From equation 2.15, we find the proportion-of-variance-accounted-for (r^2):

$$r^2 = \frac{\chi^2}{N} = \frac{4.2}{2108} = .002$$

Thus, the propranolol study was discontinued for an effect accounting for 1/5th of 1% of the variance! To display this result as a BESD we take the square root of r^2 to obtain the r we use for the BESD. That r is about .04 which displays as shown in Table 7.4. As behavioral researchers we are not accustomed to thinking of r's of .04 as reflecting effect sizes of practical importance. If we were among the 4 per 100 who moved from one outcome to the other, we might well revise our view of the practical import of small effects!

VI.C. Concluding Note on Interpreting Effect Sizes

Rosenthal and Rubin (1982c) proposed that the reporting of effect sizes could be made more intuitive and more informative by using the BESD. It was their belief that the use of the BESD to display the increase in success rate due to treatment would more clearly convey the real-world importance of treatment effects than would the commonly used descriptions of effect size, especially those based on the proportion of variance accounted for.

One effect of the routine employment of a display procedure such as the BESD to index the practical meaning of our research results would be to give us more useful and realistic assessments of how well we are doing as researchers in applied social and behavioral science and in the social and behavioral sciences more generally. Employment of the BESD has, in fact, shown that we are doing considerably better in our "softer" sciences than we thought we were.

TABLE 7.4
The Binomial Effect Size Display
for the Discontinued Propranolol Study

Condition	Treatment Result		Σ
	Alive	Dead	
Propranolol	52	48	100
Placebo	48	52	100
Σ	100	100	200

REFERENCES

Adcock, C. J. (1960). A note on combining probabilities. *Psychometrika, 25,* 303-305.

American Psychological Association. (1983). *Publication manual of the American Psychological Association* (3rd ed.). Washington, DC: Author.

Armor, D. J. (1974). Theta reliability and factor scaling. In H. L. Costner (Ed.), *Sociological methodology 1973-1974.* San Francisco: Jossey-Bass.

Bakan, D. (1967). *On method.* San Francisco: Jossey-Bass.

Birch, M. W. (1963). Maximum likelihood in three-way contingency tables. *Journal of the Royal Statistical Society, B, 25,* 220-233.

Birnbaum, A. (1954). Combining independent tests of significance. *Journal of the American Statistical Association, 49,* 559-574.

Bloom, B. S. (1964). *Stability and change in human characteristics.* New York: John Wiley.

Blyth, C. R. (1972). On Simpson's paradox and the sure-thing principle. *Journal of the American Statistical Association, 67,* 364-366.

Brehm, J. W. (1966). *A theory of psychological reactance.* New York: Academic Press.

Brozek, J., & Tiede, K. (1952). Reliable and questionable significance in a series of statistical tests. *Psychological Bulletin, 49,* 339-341.

Cochran, W. G. (1937). Problems arising in the analysis of a series of similar experiments. *Journal of the Royal Statistical Society,* Supplement 4(1), 102-118.

Cochran, W. G. (1943). The comparison of different scales of measurement for experimental results. *Annals of Mathematical Statistics, 14,* 205-216.

Cochran, W. G. (1954). Some methods for strengthening the common χ^2 tests. *Biometrics, 10,* 417-451.

Cochran, W. G., & Cox, G. M. (1957). *Experimental designs (2nd ed.).* New York: John Wiley. (First corrected printing, 1968.)

Cohen, J. (1962). The statistical power of abnormal-social psychological research: A review. *Journal of Abnormal and Social Psychology, 65,* 145-153.

Cohen, J. (1965). Some statistical issues in psychological research. In B. B. Wolman (Ed.), *Handbook of clinical psychology.* New York: McGraw-Hill.

Cohen, J. (1969). *Statistical power analysis for the behavioral sciences.* New York: Academic Press.

Cohen, J. (1977). *Statistical power analysis for the behavioral sciences (rev. ed.).* New York: Academic Press.

Compton, J. W. (1970). Experimenter bias: Reaction time and types of expectancy information. *Perceptual and Motor Skills, 31,* 159-168.

Cook, T. D., & Leviton, L. C. (1980). Reviewing the literature: A comparison of traditional methods with meta-analysis. *Journal of Personality, 48,* 449-472.

Cooper, H. M. (1979). Statistically combining independent studies: A meta-analysis of sex differences in conformity research. *Journal of Personality and Social Psychology, 37,* 131-146.

Cooper, H. M. (1981). On the significance of effects and the effects of significance. *Journal of Personality and Social Psychology, 41,* 1013-1018.

Cooper, H. M. (1982). Scientific guidelines for conducting integrative research reviews. *Review of Educational Research, 52,* 291-302.

Cooper, H. (1984). *The integrative research review: A social science approach.* Beverly Hills, CA: Sage.

Cooper, H. M., & Rosenthal, R. (1980). Statistical versus traditional procedures for summarizing research findings. *Psychological Bulletin, 87,* 442-449.

DePaulo, B. M., & Rosenthal, R. (1979). Ambivalence, discrepancy, and deception in nonverbal communication. In R. Rosenthal (Ed.), *Skill in nonverbal communication* (pp. 204-248). Cambridge, MA: Oelgeschlager, Gunn & Hain.

DePaulo, B. M., Zuckerman, M., & Rosenthal, R. (1980). Detecting deception: Modality effects. In L. Wheeler (Ed.), *Review of personality and social psychology.* Beverly Hills, CA: Sage.

Doctor, R. M. (1968). *Bias effects and awareness in studies of verbal conditioning.* Doctoral dissertation, University of Illinois.

Dusek, J. B., & Joseph, G. (1983). The bases of teacher expectancies: A meta-analysis. *Journal of Educational Psychology, 75,* 327-346.

Eagly, A. H., & Carli, L. L. (1981). Sex of researchers and sex-typed communications as determinants of sex differences in influenceability: A meta-analysis of social influence studies. *Psychological Bulletin, 90,* 1-20.

Edgington, E. S. (1972a). An additive method for combining probability values from independent experiments. *Journal of Psychology, 80,* 351-363.

Edgington, E. S. (1972b). A normal curve method for combining probability values from independent experiments. *Journal of Psychology, 82,* 85-89.

Eisner, D. A., Kosick, R. R., & Thomas, J. (1974). Investigators' instructions and experimenters' misrecording of questionnaire data. *Psychological Reports, 35,* 1278.

Elashoff, J. D. (1978). Box scores are for baseball. *The Behavioral and Brain Sciences, 3,* 392.

Ennis, J. G. (1974). *The bias effect of intentionality and expectancy on operant acquisition in rats, and on the accuracy of student experimental reports.* Unpublished manuscript, Middlebury College.

Federighi, E. T. (1959). Extended tables of the percentage points of Student's t-distribution. *Journal of the American Statistical Association, 54,* 683-688.

Feldman, K. A. (1971). Using the work of others: Some observations on reviewing and integrating. *Sociology of Education, 44,* 86-102.

Fienberg, S. E. (1977). *The analysis of cross-classified categorical data.* Cambridge, MA: The MIT Press.

Fisher, R. A. (1928). *Statistical methods for research workers (2nd ed.).* London: Oliver & Boyd.

Fisher, R. A. (1932). *Statistical methods for research workers (4th ed.).* London: Oliver & Boyd.

Fisher, R. A. (1938). *Statistical methods for research workers (7th ed.).* London: Oliver & Boyd.

Fiske, D. W. (1978). The several kinds of generalization. *The Behavioral and Brain Sciences, 3,* 393-394.

Fiske, D. W. (1983). The meta-analytic revolution in outcome research. *Journal of Consulting and Clinical Psychology, 51,* 65-70.

Fleming, E. S., & Anttonen, R. G. (1971). Teacher expectancy as related to the academic and personal growth of primary-age children. *Monographs of the Society for Research in Child Development, 36*(5, Whole No. 145).

Friedman, H. (1968). Magnitude of experimental effect and a table for its rapid estimation. *Psychological Bulletin, 70,* 245-251.

Glass, G. V (1976). Primary, secondary, and meta-analysis of research. *Educational Researcher, 5,* 3-8.

Glass, G. V (1977). Integrating findings: The meta-analysis of research. *Review of Research in Education, 5,*351-379.

Glass, G. V (1978). In defense of generalization. *The Behavioral and Brain Sciences, 3,* 394-395.

Glass, G. V (1980). Summarizing effect sizes. In R. Rosenthal (Ed.), *New directions for methodology of social and behavioral science: Quantitative assessment of research domains.* San Francisco: Jossey-Bass.

Glass, G. V, & Kliegl, R. M. (1983). An apology for research integration in the study of pyschotherapy. *Journal of Consulting and Clinical Psychology, 51,* 28-41.

Glass, G. V, McGaw, B., & Smith, M. L. (1981). *Meta-analysis in social research.* Beverly Hills, CA: Sage.

Glass, T. R. (1971). *Experimenter effects in a measure of intelligence.* Unpublished manuscript, Fairleigh Dickinson University.

Goldberg, M. (1978). *Acoustical factors in the perception of stress.* Unpublished manuscript, Harvard University, Cambridge.

Green, B. F., & Hall, J. A. (in press). Quantitative methods for literature reviews. *Annual Review of Psychology.*

Guilford, J. P. (1954). *Psychometric methods (2nd ed.).* New York: McGraw-Hill.

Guilford, J. P., & Fruchter, B. (1978). *Fundamental statistics in psychology and education (6th ed.).* New York: McGraw-Hill.

Hall, J. A. (1979). Gender, gender roles, and nonverbal communication skills. In R. Rosenthal (Ed.), *Skill in nonverbal communication: Individual differences* (pp. 32-67). Cambridge, MA: Oelgeschlager, Gunn & Hain.

Hall, J. A. (1980). Gender differences in nonverbal communication skills. In R. Rosenthal (Ed.), *New directions for methodology of social and behavioral science: Quantitative assessment of research domains* (pp. 63-77). San Francisco: Jossey-Bass.

Hawthorne, J. W. (1972). *The influence of the set and dependence of the data collector on the experimenter bias effect.* Doctoral dissertation, Duke University.

Hedges, L. V. (1981). Distribution theory for Glass's estimator of effect size and related estimators. *Journal of Educational Statistics, 6,* 107-128.

Hedges, L. V. (1982a). Estimation of effect size from a series of independent experiments. *Psychological Bulletin, 92,* 490-499.

Hedges, L. V. (1982b). Fitting categorical models to effect sizes from a series of experiments. *Journal of Educational Statistics, 7,* 119-137.

Hedges, L. V. (1982c). Fitting continuous models to effect size data. *Journal of Educational Statistics, 7,* 245-270.

Hedges, L. V. (1983a). Combining independent estimators in research synthesis. *British Journal of Mathematical and Statistical Psychology, 36*(1), 123-131.

Hedges, L. V. (1983b). A random effects model for effect sizes. *Psychological Bulletin, 93,* 388-395.

Hedges, L. V., & Olkin, I. (1980). Vote counting methods in research synthesis. *Psychological Bulletin, 88,* 359-369.

Hedges, L. V., & Olkin, I. (1982). Analyses, reanalyses, and meta-analysis. *Contemporary Education Review, 1,* 157-165.

Hedges, L. V., & Olkin, I. (1983a). Clustering estimates of effect magnitude from independent studies. *Psychological Bulletin, 93,* 563-573.

Hedges, L. V., & Olkin, I. (1983b). Regression models in research synthesis. *The American Statistician, 37,* 137-140.

Hoaglin, D. C., Mosteller, F., & Tukey, J. W. (Eds.). (1983). *Understanding robust and exploratory data analysis.* New York: John Wiley.

Howland, C. W. (1970). *The influence of knowledge of results and experimenter and subject personality styles upon the expectancy effect.* Masters thesis, University of Wisconsin.

Hsu, L. M. (1980). Tests of differences in p levels as tests of differences in effect sizes. *Psychological Bulletin, 88,* 705-708.

Hunter, J. E., Schmidt, F. L., & Jackson, G. B. (1982). *Meta-analysis: Cumulating research findings across studies.* Beverly Hills, CA: Sage.

Hyde, J. S. (1980). How large are cognitive gender differences? A meta-analysis using ω^2 and d. *American Psychologist, 36,* 892-901.

Jackson, G. B. (1978). *Methods for reviewing and integrating research in the social sciences.* (NSF Report for Grant DIS 76-20398). Washington, DC: National Science Foundation. (NTIS No. PB-283-747).

Jacob, T. (1969). *The emergence and mediation of the experimenter-bias effect as a function of "demand characteristics," experimenter "investment" and the nature of the experimental task.* Unpublished manuscript, University of Nebraska.

Johnson, R. W., & Adair, J. G. (1970). The effects of systematic recording error vs. experimenter bias on latency of word association. *Journal of Experimental Research in Personality, 4,* 270-275.

Johnson, R. W., & Adair, J. G. (1972). Experimenter expentancy vs. systematic recording error under automated and nonautomated stimulus presentation. *Journal of Experimental Research in Personality, 6,* 88-94.

Johnson, R. W., & Ryan, B. J. (1976). Observer recorder error as affected by different tasks and different expectancy inducements. *Journal of Research in Personality, 10,* 201-214.

Jones, L. V., & Fiske, D. W. (1953). Models for testing the significance of combined results. *Psychological Bulletin, 50,* 375-382.

Jung, J. (1978). Self-negating functions of self-fulfilling prophecies. *The Behavioral and Brain Sciences, 3,* 397-398.

Kaplan, A. (1964). *The conduct of inquiry: Methodology for behavioral science.* Scranton, PA: Chandler.

Kennedy, J. L., & Uphoff, H. F. (1939). Experiments on the nature of extrasensory perception: III. The recording error criticism of extra-chance scores. *Journal of Parapsychology, 3,* 226-245.

Kolata, G. B. (1981). Drug found to help heart attack survivors. *Science, 214,* 774-775.

Kraemer, H. C., & Andrews, G. (1982). A nonparametric technique for meta-analysis effect size calculation. *Psychological Bulletin, 91,* 404-412.

Krauth, J. (1983). Nonparametric effect size estimation: A comment on Kraemer and Andrews. *Psychological Bulletin, 94,* 190-192.

Kulik, J. A., Kulik, C. C., & Cohen, P. A. (1979). A meta-analysis of outcome studies of Keller's Personalized System of Instruction. *American Psychologist, 34,* 307-318.

Lamb, W. K., & Whitla, D. K. (1983). *Meta-analysis and the integration of research findings: A trend analysis and bibliography prior to 1983.* Unpublished manuscript, Harvard University, Cambridge.

Lancaster, H. O. (1961). The combination of probabilities: An application of orthonormal functions. *Australian Journal of Statistics, 3,* 20-33.

Landman, J. T., & Dawes, R. M. (1982). Psychotherapy outcome: Smith and Glass' conclusions stand up under scrutiny. *American Psychologist, 37,* 504-516.

Lewin, L. M., & Wakefield, J. A., Jr. (1979). Percentage agreement and phi: A conversion table. *Journal of Applied Behavior Analysis, 12,* 299-301.

Light, R. J. (1979). Capitalizing on variation: How conflicting research findings can be helpful for policy. *Educational Researcher, 8,* 7-11.

Light, R. J., & Pillemer, D. B. (1982). Numbers and narrative: Combining their strengths in research reviews. *Harvard Educational Review, 52,* 1-26.

Light, R. J., & Smith, P. V. (1971). Accumulating evidence: Procedures for resolving contradictions among different research studies. *Harvard Educational Review, 41,* 429-471.

Lilliefors, H. W. (1967). On the Kolmogorov-Smirnov test for normality with mean and variance unknown. *Journal of the American Statistical Association, 62,* 399-402.

Lush, J. L. (1931). Predicting gains in feeder cattle and pigs. *Journal of Agricultural Research, 42,* 853-881.

Mayo, C. C. (1972). *External conditions affecting experimental bias.* Doctoral dissertation, University of Houston.

Mayo, R. J. (1978). Statistical considerations in analyzing the results of a collection of experiments. *The Behavioral and Brain Sciences, 3,* 400-401.

Marvell, T. B. (1979). *Personal communication.* National Center for State Courts, Williamsburg, VA.

McConnell, R. A., Snowdon, R. J., & Powell, K. F. (1955). Wishing with dice. *Journal of Experimental Psychology, 50,* 269-275.

McNemar, Q. (1960). At random: Sense and nonsense. *American Psychologist, 15,* 295-300.

Mintz, J. (1983). Integrating research evidence: A commentary on meta-analysis. *Journal of Consulting and Clinical Psychology, 51,* 71-75.

Mosteller, F. M., & Bush, R. R. (1954). Selected quantitative techniques. In G. Lindzey (Ed.), *Handbook of social psychology: Vol. 1. Theory and method* (pp. 289-334). Cambridge, MA: Addison-Wesley.

Mosteller, F., & Rourke, R. E. K. (1973). *Sturdy statistics.* Reading, MA: Addison-Wesley.

Mullen, B., & Rosenthal, R. (1984). *BASIC meta-analysis programs for microcomputers.* Unpublished manuscript, Murray State University, Murray, Ky.

Pearson, K. (1933a). Appendix to Dr. Elderton's paper on "The Lanarkshire milk experiment." *Annals of Eugenics, 5,* 337-338.

Pearson, K. (1933b). On a method of determining whether a sample of size *n* supposed to have been drawn from a parent population having a known probability integral has probably been drawn at random. *Biometrika, 25,* 379-410.

Persinger, G. W., Knutson, C., & Rosenthal, R. (1968). *Communication of interpersonal expectations of ward personnel to neuropsychiatric patients.* Unpublished data, Harvard University.

Pillemer, D. B., & Light, R. J. (1980a). Benefiting from variation in study outcomes. In R. Rosenthal (Ed.), *New directions for methodology of social and behavioral science: Quantitative assessment of research domains* (pp. 1-11). San Francisco: Jossey-Bass.

Pillemer, D. B., & Light, R. J. (1980b). Synthesizing outcomes: How to use research evidence from many studies. *Harvard Educational Review, 50,* 176-195.

Prioleau, L., Murdock, M., &Brody, N. (1983). An analysis of psychotherapy vs. placebo studies. *The Behavioral and Brain Sciences, 6,* 275-310.

Rimland, B. (1979). Death knell for psychotherapy? *American Psychologist, 34,* 192.

Rosenthal, M. (1984). *Bibliographic retrieval for the social and behavioral science meta-analyst.* Unpublished manuscript.

Rosenthal, R. (1961, September). On the social psychology of the psychological experiment: With particular reference to experimenter bias. In H. W. Riecken (Chair), *On the social psychology of the psychological experiment.* Symposium conducted at the meeting of the American Psychological Association, New York.

Rosenthal, R. (1963). On the social psychology of the psychological experiment: The experimenter's hypothesis as unintended determinant of experimental results. *American Scientist, 51*, 268-283.

Rosenthal, R. (1964). Effects of the experimenter on the results of psychological research. In B. A. Maher (Ed.), *Progress in experimental personality research, Vol. 1* (pp. 79-114). New York: Academic Press.

Rosenthal, R. (1966). *Experimenter effects in behavioral research.* New York: Appleton-Century-Crofts.

Rosenthal, R. (1968a). An application of the Kolmogorov-Smirnov test for normality with estimated mean and variance. *Psychological Reports, 22*, 570.

Rosenthal, R. (1968b). Experimenter expectancy and the reassuring nature of the null hypothesis decision procedure. *Psychological Bulletin Monograph Supplement, 70*, 30-47.

Rosenthal, R. (1969). Interpersonal expectations. In R. Rosenthal and R. L. Rosnow (Eds.), *Artifact in behavioral research* (pp. 181-277). New York: Academic Press.

Rosenthal, R. (1976). *Experimenter effects in behavioral research.* Enlarged edition. New York: Irvington.

Rosenthal, R. (1978a). Combining results of independent studies. *Psychological Bulletin, 85*, 185-193.

Rosenthal, R. (1978b). How often are our numbers wrong? *American Psychologist, 33*, 1005-1008.

Rosenthal, R. (1979a). The "file drawer problem" and tolerance for null results. *Psychological Bulletin, 86*, 638-641.

Rosenthal, R. (1979b). Replications and their relative utilities. *Replications in Social Psychology, 1*(1), 15-23.

Rosenthal, R. (Ed.). (1980). *New directions for methodology of social and behavioral science: Quantitative assessment of research domains* (No. 5). San Francisco: Jossey-Bass.

Rosenthal, R. (1982a). Conducting judgment studies. In K. R. Scherer & P. Ekman (Eds.), *Handbook of methods in nonverbal behavior research* (pp. 287-361). New York: Cambridge University Press.

Rosenthal, R. (1982b). Valid interpretation of quantitative research results. In D. Brinberg & L. H. Kidder (Eds.), *Forms of validity in research* (pp. 59-75). San Francisco: Jossey-Bass.

Rosenthal, R. (1983a). Assessing the statistical and social importance of the effects of pyschotherapy. *Journal of Consulting and Clinical Psychology, 51*, 4-13.

Rosenthal, R. (1983b). Improving meta-analytic procedures for assessing the effects of psychotherapy vs. placebo. *The Behavioral and Brain Sciences, 6*, 298-299.

Rosenthal, R. (1983c). Meta-analysis: Toward a more cumulative social science. In L. Bickman (Ed.), *Applied social psychology annual* (Vol. 4) (pp. 65-93). Beverly Hills, CA: Sage.

Rosenthal, R. (1983d). Methodological issues in behavioral sciences. In B. B. Wolman (Ed.), *Progress volume I: International encyclopedia of psychiatry, psychology, psychoanalysis, & neurology* (pp. 273-277). New York: Aesculapius Publishers.

Rosenthal, R. (in press a). Designing, analyzing, interpreting, and summarizing placebo studies. In L. White, B. Tursky, & G. Schwartz (Eds.), *Placebo: Clinical phenomena and new insights.* New York: Guilford.

Rosenthal, R. (in press b). From unconscious experimenter bias to teacher expectancy effects. In J. B. Dusek, V. C. Hall, & W. J. Meyer (Eds.), *Teacher expectancies.* Hillsdale, NJ: Lawrence J. Erlbaum.

Rosenthal, R., & DePaulo, B. M. (1979). Sex differences in accommodation in nonverbal communication. In R. Rosenthal (Ed.), *Skill in nonverbal communication: Individual differences* (pp. 68-103). Cambridge, MA: Oelgeschlager, Gunn & Hain.

Rosenthal, R., Friedman, C. J., Johnson, C. A., Fode, K. L., Schill, T. R., White, C. R., & Vikan-

Kline, L. L. (1964). Variables affecting experimenter bias in a group situation. *Genetic Psychology Monographs, 70,* 271-296.

Rosenthal, R., & Gaito, J. (1963). The interpretation of levels of significance by psychological researchers. *Journal of Psychology, 55,* 33-38.

Rosenthal, R., & Gaito, J. (1964). Further evidence for the cliff effect in the interpretation of levels of significance. *Psychological Reports, 15,* 570.

Rosenthal, R., & Hall, C. M. (1968). *Computational errors in behavioral research.* Unpublished data, Harvard University.

Rosenthal, R., Hall, J. A., DiMatteo, M. R., Rogers, P. L., & Archer, D. (1979). *Sensitivity to nonverbal communication: The PONS Test.* Baltimore: The Johns Hopkins University Press.

Rosenthal, R., & Rosnow, R. L. (1975). *The volunteer subject.* New York: John Wiley.

Rosenthal, R., & Rosnow, R. L. (1984a). *Essentials of behavioral research: Methods and data analysis.* New York: McGraw-Hill.

Rosenthal, R., & Rosnow, R. L. (1984b). *Understanding behavioral science.* New York: McGraw-Hill.

Rosenthal, R., & Rosnow, R. L. (in press). *Contrasts: Focused comparisons in the analysis of variance.* New York: Cambridge University Press.

Rosenthal, R., & Rubin, D. B. (1978a). Interpersonal expectancy effects: The first 345 studies. *The Behavioral and Brain Sciences, 3,* 377-386.

Rosenthal, R., & Rubin, D. B. (1978b). Issues in summarizing the first 345 studies of interpersonal expectancy effects. *The Behavioral and Brain Sciences, 3,* 410-415.

Rosenthal, R., & Rubin, D. B. (1979a). Comparing significance levels of independent studies. *Psychological Bulletin, 86,* 1165-1168.

Rosenthal, R., & Rubin, D. B. (1979b). A note on percent variance explained as a measure of the importance of effects. *Journal of Applied Social Psychology, 9,* 395-396.

Rosenthal, R., & Rubin, D. B. (1980a). Further issues in summarizing 345 studies of interpersonal expectancy effects. *The Behavioral and Brain Sciences, 3,* 475-476.

Rosenthal, R., & Rubin, D. B. (1980b). Summarizing 345 studies of interpersonal expectancy effects. In R. Rosenthal (Ed.), *New directions for methodology of social and behavioral science: Quantitative assessment of research domains* (pp. 79-95). San Francisco: Jossey-Bass.

Rosenthal, R., & Rubin, D. B. (1982a). Comparing effect sizes of independent studies. *Psychological Bulletin, 92,* 500-504.

Rosenthal, R., & Rubin, D. B. (1982b). Further meta-analytic procedures for assessing cognitive gender differences. *Journal of Educational Psychology, 74,* 708-712.

Rosenthal, R., & Rubin, D. B. (1982c). A simple, general purpose display of magnitude of experimental effect. *Journal of Educational Psychology, 74,* 166-169.

Rosenthal, R., & Rubin, D. B. (1983). Ensemble-adjusted *p* values. *Psychological Bulletin, 94,* 540-541.

Rosenthal, R., & Rubin, D. B. (in press). *Multiple contrasts and ordered Bonferroni procedures. Journal of Educational Psychology.*

Rosnow, R. L. (1981). *Paradigms in transition.* New York: Oxford University Press.

Rusch, F. R., Greenwood, C. R., & Walker, H. M. (1978). *The effects of complexity, time and feedback upon experimenter calculation errors.* Unpublished manuscript, University of Illinois, Urbana-Champaign.

Rusch, F. R., Walker, H. M., & Greenwood, C. R. (1974). *A systematic analysis of experimenter error responses in the calculation of observation data.* Unpublished manuscript, University of Oregon, Eugene.

Shapiro, D. A., & Shapiro, D. (1983). Comparative therapy outcome research: Methodological implications of meta-analysis. *Journal of Consulting and Clinical Psychology, 51,* 42-53.

Siegel, S. (1956). *Nonparametric statistics*. New York: McGraw-Hill.

Simpson, E. H. (1951). The interpretation of interaction in contingency tables. *Journal of the Royal Statistical Society, B, 13,* 238-241.

Smart, R. G. (1964). The importance of negative results in psychological research. *Canadian Psychologist, 5a,* 225-232.

Smith, M. L. (1980). Integrating studies of psychotherapy outcomes. In R. Rosenthal (Ed.), *New directions for methodology of social and behavioral science: Quantitative assessment of research domains* (pp. 47-61). San Francisco: Jossey-Bass.

Smith, M. L., & Glass, G. V. (1977). Meta-analysis of psychotherapy outcome studies. *American Psychologist, 32,* 752-760.

Smith, M. L., Glass, G. V, & Miller, T. I. (1980). *The benefits of psychotherapy.* Baltimore: Johns Hopkins University Press.

Snedecor, G. W. (1946). *Statistical methods (4th ed.).* Ames: Iowa State College Press.

Snedecor, G. W., & Cochran, W. G. (1967). *Statistical methods (6th ed.).* Ames: Iowa State University Press.

Snedecor, G. W., & Cochran, W. G. (1980). *Statistical methods (7th ed.).* Ames: Iowa State University Press.

Sterling, T. D. (1959). Publication decisions and their possible effects on inferences drawn from tests of significance—or vice versa. *Journal of the American Statistical Association, 54,* 30-34.

Stock, W. A., Okun, M. A., Haring, M. J., Miller, W., Kinney, C., & Ceurvorst, R. W. (1982). Rigor in data synthesis: A case study of reliability in meta-analysis. *Educational Researcher, 11,* 10-14.

Stouffer, S. A., Suchman, E. A., DeVinney, L. C., Star, S. A., & Williams, R. M., Jr. (1949). *The American soldier: Adjustment during army life, Vol. I.* Princeton, NJ: Princeton University Press.

Strube, M. J., & Hartmann, D. P. (1983). Meta-analysis: Techniques, applications, and functions. *Journal of Consulting and Clinical Psychology, 51,* 14-27.

Sudman, S., & Bradburn, N. M. (1974). *Response effects in surveys. A review and synthesis.* Chicago: Aldine.

Taveggia, T. C. (1974). Resolving research controvery through empirical cumulation: Toward reliable sociological knowledge. *Sociological Methods & Research, 2,* 395-407.

Thorndike, R. L. (1933). The effect of the interval between test and retest on the constancy of the IQ. *Journal of Educational Psychology, 24,* 543-549.

Tippett, L. H. C. (1931). *The methods of statistics.* London: Williams & Norgate.

Tobias, P. (1978). *Personal communication.* Los Angeles: IBM.

Todd, J. L. (1971). *Social evaluation orientation, task orientation, and deliberate cuing in experimenter bias effect.* Doctoral dissertation, University of California, Los Angeles.

Tukey, J. W. (1977). *Exploratory data analysis.* Reading, MA: Addison-Wesley.

Underwood, B. J. (1957). Interference and forgetting. *Psychological Review, 64,* 49-60.

Upton, G. J. G. (1978). *The analysis of cross-tabulated data.* New York: John Wiley.

Viana, M. A. G. (1980). Statistical methods for summarizing independent correlational results. *Journal of Educational Statistics, 5,* 83-104.

Wakefield, J. A., Jr. (1980). Relationship between two expressions of reliability: Percentage agreement and phi. *Educational and Psychological Measurement, 40,* 593-597.

Walberg, H. J., & Haertel, E. H. (Eds.). (1980). Research integration: The state of the art. *Evaluation in Education, 4,* Whole Number 1.

Walker, H. M., & Lev, J. (1953). *Statistical inference.* New York: Holt, Rinehart & Winston.

Wallace, D. L. (1959). Bounds on normal approximations to Student's and the chi-square distributions. *Annals of Mathematical Statistics, 30,* 1121-1130.

Weiss, L. R. (1967). *Experimenter bias as a function of stimulus ambiguity.* Unpublished manuscript, State University of New York at Buffalo.

Wilkinson, B. (1951). A statistical consideration in psychological research. *Psychological Bulletin, 48,* 156-158.

Wilson, G. T., & Rachman, S. J. (1983). Meta-analysis and the evaluation of psychotherapy outcome: Limitations and liabilities. *Journal of Consulting and Clinical Psychology, 51,* 54-64.

Winer, B. J. (1971). *Statistical principles in experimental design (2nd ed.).* New York: McGraw-Hill.

Wolins, L. (1962). Responsibility for raw data. *American Psychologist, 17,* 657-658.

Yule, G. U. (1903). Notes on the theory of association of attributes in statistics. *Biometrika, 2,* 121-134.

Zelen, M., & Joel, L. S. (1959). The weighted compounding of two independent significance tests. *Annals of Mathematical Statistics, 30,* 885-895.

Zuckerman, M., DePaulo, B. M., & Rosenthal, R. (1981). Verbal and nonverbal communication of deception. In L. Berkowitz (Ed.), *Advances in Experimental Social Psychology* (Vol. 14, pp. 1-59). New York: Academic Press.

INDEX

ABOUT THE AUTHOR

Robert Rosenthal received his A.B. (1953) and Ph.D. (1956) in psychology from UCLA and is a Diplomate in Clinical Psychology. From 1957 to 1962 he taught at the University of North Dakota where he was Director of the Ph.D. program in clinical psychology. He then went to Harvard University, where since 1967 he has been Professor of Social Psychology. Professor Rosenthal's research has centered for over 25 years on the role of the self-fulfilling prophecy in everyday life and in laboratory situations. Special interests include the effects of teachers' expectations on students' intellectual and physical performance, the effects of experimenters' expectations on the results of their research, and the effects of healers' expectations on their patients' mental and physical health. His interests include the role of nonverbal communciation in both the mediation of interpersonal expectancy effects and in the relationship between female and male members of small work groups and small social groups, and also the sources of artifact in behavioral research and in various quantitative procedures. In the realm of data analysis, his special interests are in analysis of variance, contrast analysis, and meta-analysis.

Professor Rosenthal is a Fellow of the American Association for the Advancement of Science and of the American Psychological Association. With K. Fode, he received the 1960 Socio-psychological Prize of the American Association for the Advancement of Science and with L. Jacobson, the First Prize Cattell Fund Award of the A.P.A. (1967). He was a Senior Fulbright Scholar in the summer of 1972 and a Guggenheim Fellow (1973-1974). In 1979, the Massachusetts Psychological Association gave him its Distinguished Career Contribution Award. He has lectured widely in the United States and Canada as well as in Australia, England, Fiji, France, Germany, Israel, Italy, Papua New Guinea, and Switzerland. He is the author or coauthor of some two hundred articles and of many books.